SMALLPOX

DEADLY DISEASES AND EPIDEMICS

SMALLPOX

Kim R. Finer

CONSULTING EDITOR
The Late **I. Edward Alcamo**
Distinguished Teaching Professor of Microbiology,
SUNY Farmingdale

FOREWORD BY
David Heymann
World Health Organization

CHELSEA HOUSE
P U B L I S H E R S
A Haights Cross Communications Company
Philadelphia

Dedication

We dedicate the books in the DEADLY DISEASES AND EPIDEMICS series to Ed Alcamo, whose wit, charm, intelligence, and commitment to biology education were second to none.

CHELSEA HOUSE PUBLISHERS

VP, NEW PRODUCT DEVELOPMENT Sally Cheney
DIRECTOR OF PRODUCTION Kim Shinners
CREATIVE MANAGER Takeshi Takahashi
MANUFACTURING MANAGER Diann Grasse

Staff for Smallpox

ASSOCIATE EDITOR Beth Reger
PRODUCTION EDITOR Megan Emery
PHOTO EDITOR Sarah Bloom
SERIES DESIGNER Terry Mallon
COVER DESIGNER Keith Trego
LAYOUT 21st Century Publishing and Communications, Inc.

A Haights Cross Communications Company

http://www.chelseahouse.com

First Printing

1 3 5 7 9 8 6 4 2

Library of Congress Cataloging-in-Publication Data

Finer, Kim Renee, 1956–
  Smallpox/Kim R. Finer.
    p. cm. — (Deadly diseases and epidemics)
  ISBN 0-7910-7594-X
  1. Smallpox. I. Title. II. Series.
RA644.S6F566 2004
616.9'12—dc22

                                        2004001946

Table of Contents

Foreword

In the 1960s, many of the infectious diseases that had terrorized generations were tamed. After a century of advances, the leading killers of Americans both young and old were being prevented with new vaccines or cured with new medicines. The risk of death from pneumonia, tuberculosis (TB), meningitis, influenza, whooping cough, and diphtheria declined dramatically. New vaccines lifted the fear that summer would bring polio, and a global campaign was on the verge of eradicating smallpox worldwide. New pesticides like DDT cleared mosquitoes from homes and fields, thus reducing the incidence of malaria, which was present in the southern United States and which remains a leading killer of children worldwide. New technologies produced safe drinking water and removed the risk of cholera and other water-borne diseases. Science seemed unstoppable. Disease seemed destined to all but disappear.

But the euphoria of the 1960s has evaporated.

The microbes fought back. Those causing diseases like TB and malaria evolved resistance to cheap and effective drugs. The mosquito developed the ability to defuse pesticides. New diseases emerged, including AIDS, Legionnaires, and Lyme disease. And diseases which had not been seen in decades re-emerged, as the hantavirus did in the Navajo Nation in 1993. Technology itself actually created new health risks. The global transportation network, for example, meant that diseases like West Nile virus could spread beyond isolated regions and quickly become global threats. Even modern public health protections sometimes failed, as they did in 1993 in Milwaukee, Wisconsin, resulting in 400,000 cases of the digestive system illness cryptosporidiosis. And, more recently, the threat from smallpox, a disease believed to be completely eradicated, has returned along with other potential bioterrorism weapons such as anthrax.

The lesson is that the fight against infectious diseases will never end.

In our constant struggle against disease, we as individuals have a weapon that does not require vaccines or drugs, and that is the warehouse of knowledge. We learn from the history of science that "modern" beliefs can be wrong. In this series of books, for example, you will learn that diseases like syphilis were once thought to be caused by eating potatoes. The invention of the microscope set science on the right path. There are more positive lessons from history. For example, smallpox was eliminated by vaccinating everyone who had come in contact with an infected person. This "ring" approach to smallpox control is still the preferred method for confronting an outbreak, should the disease be intentionally reintroduced.

At the same time, we are constantly adding new drugs, new vaccines, and new information to the warehouse. Recently, the entire human genome was decoded. So too was the genome of the parasite that causes malaria. Perhaps by looking at the microbe and the victim through the lens of genetics we will be able to discover new ways to fight malaria, which remains the leading killer of children in many countries.

Because of advances in our understanding of such diseases as AIDS, entire new classes of anti-retroviral drugs have been developed. But resistance to all these drugs has already been detected, so we know that AIDS drug development must continue.

Education, experimentation, and the discoveries that grow out of them are the best tools to protect health. Opening this book may put you on the path of discovery. I hope so, because new vaccines, new antibiotics, new technologies, and, most importantly, new scientists are needed now more than ever if we are to remain on the winning side of this struggle against microbes.

David Heymann
Executive Director
Communicable Diseases Section
World Health Organization
Geneva, Switzerland

1

Elimination of a Dreadful Scourge

On December 9, 1979, a **World Health Organization** (**WHO**) panel convened in Geneva, Switzerland, to ceremoniously sign a parchment emblazoned with a red wax seal. The proclamation, in five languages, read: "We the members of the global commission for the certification of smallpox **eradication**, certify that smallpox has been eradicated from the world." With that announcement, a **scourge** that had caused untold misery to humankind for the past 3,000 years had been conquered.

AN IDEA TAKES ROOT

The idea of global smallpox eradication traces back to Professor Victor Zhdanov, the vice minister of health of the USSR. At the 1958 meeting at the eleventh World Health Assembly in Minneapolis, Minnesota, Professor Zhdanov gave an impassioned speech on eradicating smallpox from the world. He championed vaccination as a way of containing epidemics, but scientists were skeptical about this approach.

Major WHO programs aimed at eradicating disease were nothing new; at the time, programs to eliminate both yellow fever and malaria were under way, but unfortunately, neither was showing much success. To add smallpox to eradication efforts would require funds that were not readily available. Therefore, the goal of eradicating smallpox was greeted less than enthusiastically by many countries that had limited funds to spare. With an initial budget of only $100,000 a year, the smallpox project appeared to be doomed to failure from the start.

Despite the atmosphere of pessimism, the assembly reconvened in 1959 and agreed that a global smallpox eradication program should be undertaken, with an initial strategy of vaccinating or revaccinating 80% of the world's population against smallpox.

WHY SMALLPOX?

Since the eradication programs for malaria and yellow fever seemed to be floundering, what was it about smallpox that suggested eradication of that disease would be any more successful? Several characteristics of smallpox made it an ideal target for eradication:

- Smallpox was a disease that affected only humans, with no **animal reservoir**—(unlike malaria and yellow fever, which are transmitted by mosquitoes).

- When smallpox affected unvaccinated individuals, the disease was **acute** (rapid onset, severe symptoms, and short duration) and was contagious only when a rash was visible.

- An effective **vaccine** against the one stable **strain** of the **virus** was available and had been in use for over 100 years.

- Anyone infected either died from the disease or recovered with lifelong immunity; consequently, there was no **carrier** state that could make transmission unpredictable.

- There was no social stigma associated with the disease— (unlike leprosy or a sexually transmitted disease, where many patients tried to hide their affliction).

Even Dr. Edward Jenner, who in 1796 carried out the first smallpox vaccination, recognized the potential to eradicate the disease. Speaking on vaccination, Dr. Jenner declared:

It now becomes too manifest to admit of controversy that the annihilation of smallpox, the most dreadful scourge of the human species, must be the result of this practice.

CARRYING OUT THE PLAN

Although the resolution for global eradication of smallpox was passed in 1959, the program was slow to start and to gain momentum. However, between 1965 and 1968, several advances made the goal of eradication more realistic. During this time, the WHO yearly budget for smallpox eradication increased to $2.5 million, a much more realistic budget for such a large undertaking. A stable, freeze-dried vaccine also became commercially available, which made it easier to transport and store the vaccine in hot, humid climates. Another simple but significant advance was the introduction of the **bifurcated** needle for vaccination (see Chapter 4). Previously, jet injection guns had been used (Figure 1.1), but these often broke down and needed servicing. Each jet injection used approximately 0.01 ml of vaccine per dose. Unlike the gun, the needles used only 0.0025 ml of vaccine per dose, required no maintenance, and were easily sterilized. As an added bonus, a local worker could be trained in 10 to 15 minutes to use the bifurcated needle to correctly administer a vaccination. By 1967, with Dr. Donald A. Henderson (Figure 1.2) heading the WHO's intensified global eradication program, efforts began to pay off and success was realized.

A NEW BATTLE STRATEGY

While initially focusing on mass vaccination, the eradication campaign eventually evolved into a program of **surveillance** and **containment**. This strategy involved tracking smallpox outbreaks and containing them by using the smallpox vaccine to immunize everyone in a ring around the outbreak. But why change the primary strategy to one of surveillance-containment rather than mass vaccination?

Early in the program, after several months of vaccinating, it became clear that attempting to vaccinate 80% of a population was going to be nearly impossible. Even in areas that achieved the 80% vaccination level, cases of smallpox were still occurring.

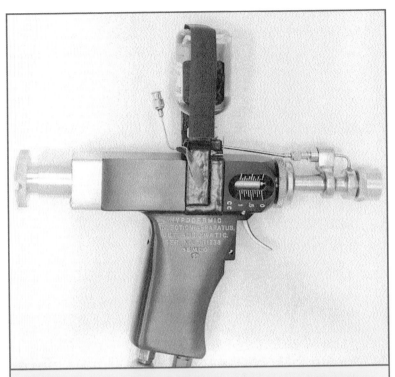

Figure 1.1 The smallpox vaccine was initially administered using a jet injection gun, pictured here. Although the gun could be used to vaccinate many people in a short period of time, it often broke down in the field and was difficult to repair.

A new vaccination strategy had to be found. Surveillance and containment, or building a "**firewall**" of vaccination around **infection clusters**, proved much more efficient and economical. Several early success stories supported the new strategy (see "The Development of Surveillance-Containment" on Page 13). By July 1968, surveillance-containment had become the primary strategy in the fight to eradicate smallpox.

Surveillance-containment required two major components: actively seeking out cases of smallpox, and vaccinating all people who came into contact with the infected person. Workers searched for cases town by town and house by house. Rewards

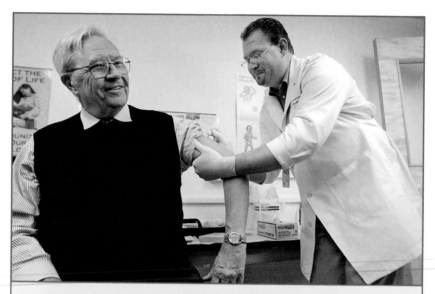

Figure 1.2 Dr. Donald A. Henderson (left) was working for the Centers for Disease Control and Prevention (CDC) when he was asked to serve as the chief of the smallpox eradication unit for the World Health Organization. He headed the WHO Intensified Smallpox Eradication Program as chief medical officer from 1966 to 1977. In 2003, due to the concern that smallpox might resurface, Dr. Henderson received the vaccine himself.

were offered to help identify cases. Once a case was identified, guards were posted at the affected dwelling. All contacts and visitors were vaccinated. The strategy worked most of the time, although two scenarios (in Africa and India) presented special challenges.

Smallpox cases among some nomadic tribes in Africa were difficult to monitor and track down. Often, people in these groups were infected with the virus causing **variola minor** (see Chapter 6 for more detail), resulting in a mild, nonlethal form of the disease that allowed infected people to remain active, travel with their groups, and spread disease. However, even these cases were eventually tracked down and eliminated as sources of infection.

THE DEVELOPMENT OF SURVEILLANCE-CONTAINMENT

Although mass vaccination initially was the official strategy of the smallpox eradication campaign, an alternative approach eventually proved to be successful. Three significant experiences demonstrated that surveillance-containment was more effective and less costly than mass vaccination.

- In October 1966, Dr. Bill Foege was working on the smallpox program in eastern Nigeria as civil war was closing in and a smallpox outbreak was occurring. Unfortunately, he was short on vaccine and personnel, so he decided to ring vaccinate, or build a barrier of containment around the outbreak. With less than 50% of his population vaccinated, he succeeded in eliminating smallpox from the region.

- The WHO provided Dr. A.R. Rao, who ran a smallpox hospital outside of Madras, India, with only enough funds to equip one team to investigate and control all outbreaks in Tamil Nadu, a state with 40 million people. In 1968, by employing surveillance-containment, Dr. Rao's team succeeded in stopping transmission in this populous region in less than one year.

- Dr. Ciro de Quadros, working seven days a week in Paraná State in Brazil with his driver and a vaccinator, eliminated smallpox from a state with a population of 7 million in less than two years (1969–1970) by using the surveillance-containment method.

Even with these dramatic success stories, it is interesting to note that many smallpox campaign administrators and workers were still not persuaded that surveillance-containment was more effective than mass vaccination.

Another challenge presented itself in India, where very large numbers of people moved from place to place on a regular basis. Also, the Hindu population of India revered Shitala Mata, the Hindu goddess of smallpox (see Chapter 2). According to Hindu beliefs, the goddess bestowed a blessing upon people by giving them smallpox. Being vaccinated against the disease was to deny those blessings. The challenge, which the eradication team met, was to demonstrate to the village leaders that the vaccine was safe and neither physical harm nor the goddess's wrath would come to those who received it.

SUCCESS

To the great delight of the WHO health workers, their efforts using surveillance and containment gradually paid off. Country after country was declared free of smallpox, and, by 1973, only six countries still reported cases of smallpox among their populations. The bad news was that these countries included some of the most heavily populated regions in the world. Three of these countries—India, Pakistan, and Bangladesh—had a combined population of 700 million.

The eradication program shifted into overdrive, and guards were posted to prevent patients in these countries from leaving their homes. Everyone within 5 miles of an infected village was vaccinated. In 1975, smallpox swept through 500 villages in Bangladesh. But the prevention methods were working, and the containment rings were tightening. By the fall of 1977, smallpox was eradicated from Bangladesh (see Figure 1.3 for a world map detailing eradication dates).

Finally, only Ethiopia continued to report cases of smallpox. Despite a civil war, famine, and torrential rains, the eradication program pressed on. It was 1976, and the end was in sight. But just when victory was at hand, smallpox broke out in neighboring Somalia. Now a campaign involving 200,000 health workers, 55 countries, and hundreds of millions of dollars focused on a hospital cook named Ali Maow Maalin. Maalin developed the

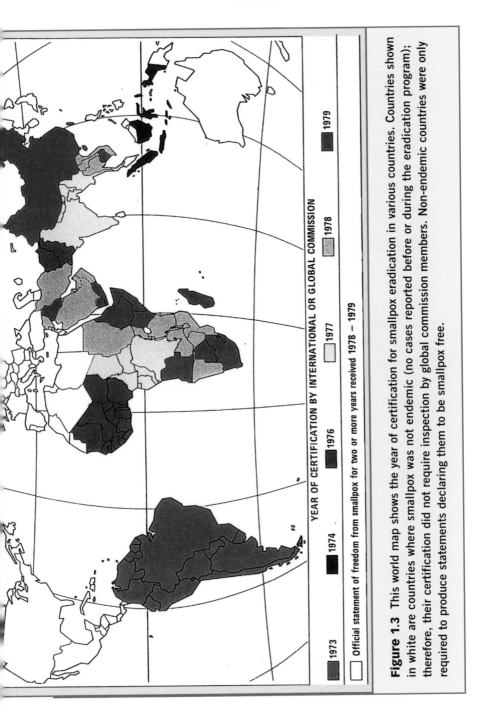

YEAR OF CERTIFICATION BY INTERNATIONAL OR GLOBAL COMMISSION

1973   1974   1976   1977   1978   1979

Official statement of freedom from smallpox for two or more years received 1978 – 1979

Figure 1.3 This world map shows the year of certification for smallpox eradication in various countries. Countries shown in white are countries where smallpox was not endemic (no cases reported before or during the eradication program); therefore, their certification did not require inspection by global commission members. Non-endemic countries were only required to produce statements declaring them to be smallpox free.

smallpox rash on October 26, 1977. Although Maalim was initially misdiagnosed (because he had already been vaccinated), he was eventually isolated, and 161 of his contacts were monitored. Maalim recovered, and none of the 161 people he came into contact with developed smallpox.

Exactly 12 years, 9 months, and 26 days after the WHO accepted a policy of intensified global eradication, the declaration that the goal had been reached was signed on December 9, 1979. Indeed, no one has experienced smallpox since that epic date.

THE MOST IMPRESSIVE ACHIEVEMENT IN MEDICAL HISTORY

The eradication of smallpox is arguably the most impressive achievement in medical history. No claim of eradication has ever been made for any other disease, and nowhere have the benefits of a public health effort been as evident. Indeed, an estimated 50 million people would have suffered a horrible sickness and death were it not for the work of Dr. Henderson's team. It is clear that surveillance-containment worked. The firewall held.

One might then ask, why study smallpox? Two reasons come to mind: One is philosophical, the second practical. The philosophical reason is that to know where you are, you must know where you have been. In other words, to understand the infectious diseases of our day, we must be familiar with the diseases that afflicted our ancestors. The lessons we have learned from smallpox are great: How people react to disease, how diseases spread, how history is intimately connected to disease, and, of course, how epidemics can be contained. Knowing these lessons helps doctors and researchers fulfill their missions in our era.

The practical reason is more sobering. With the eradication of smallpox in 1977, vaccination ended, and the world's population has since lost most of its resistance to smallpox.

This fact has not gone unnoticed by **bioterrorists**. Working outside the bounds of common decency, bioterrorists have investigated using the smallpox virus to spread fear, panic, and disease. As we shall see in the chapters ahead, the smallpox virus could be a potent weapon in the hands of terrorists, and the 21st-century world is rushing to learn all it can about how to respond to a possible smallpox epidemic that could be unleashed. It is ironic that one of the great achievements of the 20th century, the eradication of smallpox, has created such a practical problem for the 21st century.

2

History's Great Slate-Wiper

No one is certain where smallpox began, just as no one can be sure who had history's first case of plague or, in the modern era, the first case of acquired immunodeficiency syndrome (AIDS). Nevertheless, science historians are eager to know the origins of the disease as well as its historical impact. These historians have searched the writings of ancient civilizations to find mention of diseases and how they influenced society, they have studied the patterns of life through the ages to see when epidemics occurred, and they have charted the course of more recent history to see infectious disease change the pattern of living.

Their studies led to the profound conclusion that smallpox has impacted the course of human civilization as much as, or perhaps even more than, plague, malaria, influenza, cholera, syphilis, and the other great diseases of history. Such diseases are often referred to as "slate-wipers" because they travel back and forth over populations, wiping out great swaths of humanity like so many words wiped off a chalkboard with an eraser. Indeed, some medical historians believe that smallpox killed more people throughout history than anything else.

ORIGINS OF SMALLPOX

No scientist was present to record the epic date in history when the smallpox virus first infected humans, but best-guess estimates indicate that the virus was once a harmless poxvirus that infected domestic animals in Asia and Africa (the cowpox virus of cows is an example). Then, perhaps because farmers were constantly in touch with the virus, it **mutated** to a form that could thrive and replicate in human tissues. Such a scenario is not as far-fetched as it seems; research evidence presented by Beatrice Hahn in 1999 indicates that the human immunodeficiency virus (HIV) resided in African chimpanzees before it made the jump to humans. A similar process could have occurred with smallpox, perhaps about 10,000 B.C.

EARLY EVIDENCE

The earliest generally agreed-upon evidence that humans had become infected with the smallpox virus comes from ancient Egypt. Three mummies from the 18th and 20th Egyptian dynasties (1570–1085 B.C.) show scarring that appears very similar to what one would expect from smallpox. Pharaoh Ramses V (Figure 2.1), who ruled Egypt from 1161 B.C. until his death in 1157 B.C., also appears to have been a smallpox victim (see Page 21).

During the first millennium B.C., smallpox was apparently spread by wars and trade caravans throughout the Far East and northeast Africa. The Huns were believed to have carried the smallpox virus to all the areas they conquered (in China, the disease was called Hunpox). Alexander the Great's army helped spread the disease in the 4th century B.C. Alexander's soldiers are known to have introduced (or perhaps reintroduced) smallpox to India around 325 B.C.

Smallpox has both historical and religious significance in India. Hindus worshiped Shitala Mata (cool one), the goddess of smallpox (Figure 2.2). The goddess, dressed in red, is depicted riding atop a donkey. She carries a broom in

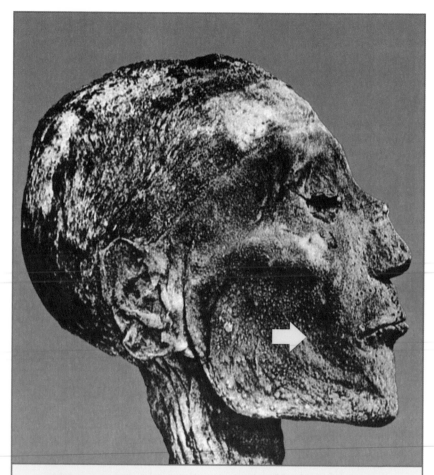

Figure 2.1 Pharaoh Ramses V ruled Egypt from 1161 to 1157 B.C. and is believed to have died from smallpox. On his face one can see lesions (arrow) that closely resemble those that develop during smallpox.

one hand to sweep away the disease, and in the other she holds a pail of water to cool her victims. Shitala Mata's feast day was celebrated by avoiding heat, which meant giving up cooking for a day and eating only cool foods and drinking cool beverages.

NATIONS OF THE WORLD

Neither Greece nor Rome escaped the horrible disease. Thucydides, the great Greek historian, wrote of an epidemic of smallpox in 430 B.C. The epidemic, which originated in Ethiopia and arrived in Greece by sea, caused lawlessness and the breakdown of civilization in Athens. He also noted that the gods seemed to have little to do with the course of the epidemic (neither being the cause of, nor able to cure, the disease). Rome suffered a serious epidemic in

PHARAOH RAMSES V

The mummy of Pharaoh Ramses V, discovered in Egypt in 1898 and since held in the Cairo Museum, appears to provide physical evidence of the early incidence of smallpox. In 1979, permission was granted by then-Egyptian President Anwar Sadat for Dr. D.R. Hopkins to examine the remains of the pharaoh. The examination revealed a rash of raised, yellow blisters 2 to 4 mm in diameter (approximately the size of a pencil point) on the face, neck, shoulders, and arms. No rash appeared on the upper abdomen or chest. This characteristic pattern of the smallpox rash as well as the appearance of the lesions is fairly diagnostic for the disease.

Electron microscopy of the wrappings from the mummy was unable to detect the smallpox virus. Unfortunately, microscopic examination of the lesions was not permitted. It is interesting to note that Pharaoh Ramses, who ruled only four years, was not buried until two years after his death, although internment typically took place 70 days following death. Scientists speculate that Ramses may have remained infectious after death and transmitted the disease to others who then died and were prevented from carrying out the burial process.

Figure 2.2 Shitala Mata, the Hindu goddess of smallpox (pictured here), is usually depicted riding atop a donkey, carrying a jar of water to cool her smallpox victims and a broom to sweep away the disease.

the second century A.D., with the most notable victim being Emperor Marcus Aurelius.

The first recorded outbreak of the epidemic in Arabia was in A.D. 570, when an army under the command of Abrah Ashram traveled from Yemen to attack Mecca. The goal of Ashram's army was to destroy the sacred shrine of the Arabs. The Qur'an (Koran) describes the battle as being won by "God," who sent birds to pelt the invading army with stones, producing pustules that spread like a pestilence. As armies of invaders swept across Northern Africa, Asia, and Europe, the scourge of smallpox seemed to follow. When Arabs captured Tripoli (in present-day Libya) in A.D. 647, they brought smallpox with them. Smallpox came to Spain when the country was invaded by the Muslim Moors of northwest Africa in A.D. 710. The Moors then crossed the Pyrenees into France in A.D. 731, bringing smallpox to the French.

New waves of smallpox were reintroduced to Europe by the Crusaders, who became infected while attempting to recapture the Holy Lands from the Arabs between A.D. 1096 and 1291. By the 1400s, smallpox had become **endemic** in Europe (a small number of cases always present), with increased numbers of cases, or epidemics, sweeping through the population every five to seven years. Smallpox was not called by this name until the 1500s so it could be differentiated from syphilis, known then as the "great pox," another scourge of the period.

According to historians, by the 1700s, almost half a million people were dying of smallpox in Europe each year. It was during this time that four reigning monarchs died of the disease: Emperor Joseph I of Austria, Tsar Peter II of Russia, King Louis XV of France, and William II of Orange. Rather than wars or family feuds, it was smallpox that had the most significant effect on European lines of succession during this period.

EARLY THERAPIES

In A.D. 910, the Persian-born physician Rhazes published the first accurate clinical description of smallpox, which was widely read by European scholars and practitioners. In his book, Rhazes also described a treatment in which he prescribed bleeding to cool the blood and sweat therapy to rid the patient of excess humors (body fluids that were believed to influence an individual's general state of health). He also believed red objects would assist treatment. Many European doctors adopted Rhazes's therapeutic approach.

When Prince John, the son of Edward II of Great Britain, fell ill with smallpox in 1314, he was covered with red blankets in a room hung with red curtains, and made to suck the red juice of a pomegranate and gargle with red mulberry wine. The prince survived. Twenty-nine-year-old Queen Elizabeth I of England also received red treatment during her battle with smallpox in 1562. She, too, survived (no thanks to red treatment), but was left with facial scars and little hair covering her head.

Unfortunately, neither the therapy of Rhazes nor any other treatments of the time had any effect on the course of smallpox. Tens of thousands continued to die as the great slate-wiper tightened its grip on the world. Loosening that grip would have to wait until the end of the 1700s.

During the 1700s, Europeans considered smallpox to be a childhood disease. Writers of the period report that one of every three English children died of smallpox before reaching the age of four. Many other children were blinded by it, and most children were pockmarked for life. But while they were ravaged by the disease, these survivors did not have to fear being stricken again, because surviving an attack of smallpox granted them lifetime immunity from the disease.

Before discussing remarkable early attempts at preventing

smallpox, we will examine how the disease that affected thousands in Europe, Asia, and Africa was transported to the New World, where it decimated the native populations in North, Central, and South America.

3

Smallpox in the Americas

When George Washington and his brother Lawrence set sail from Virginia to the island of Barbados late in September 1751, they had high hopes that Lawrence, who suffered from consumption (now referred to as tuberculosis), would find a cure, or at least relief in the warm climate and salty sea breezes. Unfortunately, the journey that was only supposed to take a week proved to be difficult as the crew battled high seas caused by a nearby storm. The ship finally landed on November 2, 1751, in Bridgetown, Barbados. As was the custom in those days, the brothers were invited to have dinner the next evening with a distant relative, Gedney Clarke. George was hesitant to go because, as he put it, "The smallpox was in his family."

Two weeks later, George's concern was realized when he wrote in his diary that he was "strongly attacked with the small Pox." George began his battle with the disease and would not write again in his diary until December 12, almost four weeks later. George eventually left Barbados and went home to recover fully from his bout with smallpox. Unfortunately, Lawrence found no relief for his tuberculosis in Barbados and eventually died on July 26, 1752, shortly after returning to his home in Mount Vernon, Virginia.

Twenty-three years later, George Washington would take command of the Continental Army in the War of Independence. General Washington, who had been left with only minor scars from his case of smallpox, knew from his experience in Barbados that he would be fighting not only the British but also another formidable foe, smallpox, which was sweeping through Boston at the time.

SMALLPOX COMES TO THE NEW WORLD

As Europeans sought out new worlds to conquer and explore, they brought their culture, language, and goods with them, and their diseases as well—including smallpox. In 1492, more than one million Arawak natives lived on the island of Hispaniola in the West Indies. By 1518, nearly one-third of the Arawak population was dead, most of them victims of smallpox brought by Christopher Columbus and his sailors. From Hispaniola, the virus traveled via infected slaves and sailors to Cuba and Puerto Rico, again killing many of the natives on those islands.

In 1519, the Spanish explorer Hernán Cortés traveled to Mexico, lured by tales of gold and other riches. Upon the Spaniards' arrival in Tenochtitlán, the Aztec capital, the Aztecs welcomed the visitors, believing that Cortés and his men were descendents of an Aztec god. Cortés repaid the Aztec kindness by imprisoning the emperor Montezuma and demanding a ransom in gold. Cortés was temporarily distracted when he heard that another Spanish conquistador, Panfilio de Narváez, had landed on the coast of Mexico. During the course of putting down his rival (Cortés had no desire to share the captured gold), one of Cortés's men contracted smallpox from a slave serving Narváez's army. Upon returning to Tenochtitlán, the soldier transmitted the virus to the very vulnerable Aztec population (Figure 3.1). Within weeks, the Aztec population was devastated by the unseen enemy— smallpox. The great Aztec Empire was defeated by a foe it never knew existed.

The Incan Empire was likewise decimated when smallpox, in two separate outbreaks, made the empire vulnerable by killing over one-third of the natives. The weakened and depopulated Incas were no match for the conquering army of Francisco Pizarro in 1533.

By the end of the 1500s, the Aztec, Incan, and Mayan nations were battered into submission. Native leaders succumbed to the

Figure 3.1 This illustration, entitled *Entrance of Cortés Into Mexico* depicts Montezuma, the Aztec emperor, greeting the Spanish explorer. The Europeans unknowingly brought smallpox to the New World, where it infected and killed many in the susceptible Aztec population.

invaders and dutifully obeyed the commands of landowners, tax collectors, and missionaries. The natives thought that divine and natural orders had spoken out loudly against their beliefs. By one historian's account, there were 25 million Native Americans when the Spanish arrived in 1520. At the end of the century, only 6 million survived.

Years later in South America, Jesuit missionaries unknowingly promoted the transmission of smallpox and death among the native Indians of Brazil. In an effort to convert the natives to Christianity, the Jesuits coerced them into living in crowded settlements where they would be baptized and live as Christians. Unfortunately, these settlements provided the perfect opportunity for the virus to spread through the population and claim many victims.

Between 1660 and 1670, approximately 64,000 native Brazilians became casualties of smallpox.

NORTH AMERICAN SCOURGE

The Indian population of North America fared no better than that of South and Central America. As Europeans settled on the continent, so too did smallpox. The first epidemic struck a group of Native Americans living near the Plymouth Colony in Massachusetts, resulting in 90% mortality. That epidemic was quickly followed by one affecting the Huron tribe near Lake Ontario in 1636 and a devastating outbreak among the Iroquois in upper New York State in 1679. Many more tribes eventually fell victim to smallpox introduced by trappers, explorers, soldiers, or settlers.

NATIVE AMERICAN CASUALTIES

In addition to acquiring smallpox infection naturally by contact with other infected humans, Native Americans may have been one of the first groups to experience the purposeful use of a biological material as a weapon (see the box on Page 30).

Why were Native Americans in all parts of the New World so susceptible to smallpox? Although no definitive answer is available, some generally agreed-upon explanations help us understand the extreme consequences that Native Americans suffered from smallpox infection.

Unlike European settlers, Native Americans were "virgin" populations, meaning they had never experienced the small-pox virus before and, therefore, no one had any sort of resistance, or **immunity**, to the disease. In Europe, the disease typically affected children because the adult population had some degree of immunity from previous exposure. In Native American populations, the disease affected both young and old. When a smallpox epidemic swept through a tribe, few adults were available to provide food, water, or nursing care to the ill or dying. Starvation and dehydration added to the mortality rate.

Genetic factors may also have contributed to the susceptibility and high mortality among Native Americans. American Indians are a genetically homogenous population compared to Europeans. This lack of **genetic diversity** may have prevented **natural selection** from exerting an influence on population survival by selecting for genes that would provide some degree of resistance to smallpox infection. So while the virus was

EARLY USE OF A BIOLOGICAL WEAPON

In 1763, Sir Jeffrey Amherst, commander of British forces in the American colonies, became concerned over the frequent attacks on his troops by Native Americans. In a July 7 correspondence with one of his colonels, Henry Bouquet, Amherst wrote, "Could it not be Contrived to Send the Small Pox among those Disaffected Tribes of Indians?" The colonel wrote back on July 13, "I will try to inoculate the _____[1] with Some Blankets that may fall in their Hands and take care not to get the disease myself." Amherst wrote back, "You will do well to try to Inoculate the Indians by means of blankets, as well as Try Every other Methode, that can serve to Extirpate this Execrable Race."

Was this act of biowarfare carried out and ultimately successful? No other correspondence between the two men exists that would point to the outcome. However, historical records do tell us that an outbreak of smallpox occurred later that year among the Mingoe, Delaware, and Shawanoe tribes of the region, killing between 60 and 80 individuals. Was it a coincidence or the result of intentional infection?

1. Bouquet drew a line in his note instead of naming the Indian tribe. He may have done this to hide his plan from his clerk. Amherst to Bouquet. Bouquet Letters, MSS 21634, British Library, London.

mutating to become more virulent, the host population was not responding with concomitant genetic selection for those traits that would allow survival of the host.

Native American healing traditions may also have contributed to the high mortality rate of smallpox. The practice of using sweat lodges exacerbated the impact of the smallpox fever. In addition, purging and fasting may have weakened the victims, contributing to their high mortality rate.

COLONISTS DO BATTLE

In North America, smallpox was not prevalent among colonists so long as their settlements remained scattered. The smallpox virus was spread among individuals when they came in contact with one another; therefore, living in settlements that were far apart from each other helped limit the spread of this disease. In some isolated settlements, smallpox was unknown for whole generations.

The colonists would soon lose their advantage, however, as their communities expanded and joined with one another. Soon, outbreaks of smallpox occurred regularly, and individuals on both sides of the Atlantic sought ways to protect themselves.

Although many North American colonists had immunity against smallpox because of childhood exposure, the disease still managed to sweep through the larger colonial cities every few years. Boston endured six major smallpox epidemics between 1636 and 1698, with another, more devastating epidemic coming in 1721. It was during this epidemic that Cotton Mather (Figure 3.2), pastor of Boston's North Church, wrote, "The grievous calamity of smallpox has now entered the town." By the 1750s, the colonists had begun to develop strategies to control the spread of smallpox. These strategies included isolation. The Puritan settlers of the Massachusetts Bay Colony quarantined ships arriving from Barbados. In South Carolina, sentinels were posted outside any home housing an infected citizen and the occupants were required to

Figure 3.2 Cotton Mather (1663–1728) was a prominent Boston minister from a well-respected New England Puritan family. In addition to studying for the ministry at Harvard, he also studied science and medicine. His strong promotion and support of variolation raised the ire of many Boston residents in 1721.

post notices to warn others of the contagion. "Pest" Island (near present-day Newport) was used by Rhode Island residents to isolate infected members of the population. Pennsylvania was one of the few British colonies that had no quarantine regulations in place in the 1770s. When the British fled Boston in 1776, General George Washington was hesitant to let his soldiers enter the city for fear of smallpox. Washington, who was cautious due to his own personal experience with smallpox, at first let only 1,000 soldiers who had already had smallpox as children enter the city. Washington was among those who were beginning to understand that, once a person had suffered from (and survived) a bout of smallpox, he or she would never get the disease again. This understanding led to early attempts at **variolation**, and eventually vaccination.

4

Developing the Smallpox Vaccine

Smallpox would not significantly be controlled around the world until the advent of vaccination, a development that was about to debut at the turn of the new century (1800). The principle of vaccination was derived from the ancient practice of variolation—inducing immunity in an otherwise susceptible individual.

VARIOLATION, AN EARLY ATTEMPT AT PROTECTION

In one type of variolation (see the box on Page 35), the smallpox virus is purposefully introduced into scratches in the skin. The principle behind variolation is to give the patient an active case of smallpox resulting in mild disease and subsequent long-lasting immunity. The practice of variolation came to North America from at least two sources: the Reverend Cotton Mather and Lady Mary Montagu, wife of the British ambassador to Turkey.

Cotton Mather Challenges Colonial Thinking

Cotton Mather, who learned of the process from his African slave Onesimus, encouraged Dr. Zabdiel Boylston to attempt variolation during the Boston smallpox epidemic of 1721. The experiment caused a public outcry. Mather's house was firebombed and Dr. Boylston was accused of spreading the infection rather than protecting individuals from it. Indeed, an outbreak in 1767 among college students traveling to Williamsburg was directly attributed to variolation. Unfortunately, two of the three students died, and local magistrates temporarily put a halt to the procedure.

Benjamin Franklin was a strong proponent of variolation. As the editor of the *Pennsylvania Gazette*, he vigorously promoted the process and helped change the public's attitude about it; consequently, Philadelphia became a center for variolation for residents of the eastern states.

Inoculation Parties Inspired by Lady Mary Montagu

In 1716, Lady Mary Montagu (Figure 4.1), wife of the British ambassador to Turkey, sent a notable letter to her friends in England. Her letter described a Turkish practice in which people protected themselves against smallpox by intentionally giving themselves the disease. Turkish citizens would open a small wound in their arms and insert a tiny drop of pus from a smallpox patient. Then they tied walnut shells over the infection sites and isolated themselves until the disease appeared.

VARIOLATION OR VACCINATION?

Variolation is a word derived from *variola*, the term for "smallpox." Variolation is the purposeful use of the smallpox virus to induce smallpox in individuals. Following a mild case of the disease (if all goes well), the patient will recover with lifelong immunity to the smallpox virus.

Variolation was performed in a number of ways. The Chinese inhaled preparations of dried smallpox scabs, while Turkish practitioners inoculated dry or pustular material into cuts on the arm of the recipient.

Vaccination is derived from the word *vacca*, which is Latin for "cow." In the process of vaccination, the patient is inoculated with material from cowpox lesions, or vaccinia. The resulting minor infection of cowpox will induce immunity to smallpox (for approximately 10 years), as well as other viruses of the orthopoxvirus genus.

Figure 4.1 Lady Montagu, shown here, was the wife of the British ambassador to Turkey. In Turkey (1716–1719), Lady Montagu learned of the practice of variolation. Having had a brother die of smallpox, and being a victim herself (she was left with no eyelashes and facial pockmarks), she knew the grave consequences of developing natural smallpox. While in Turkey, she had her son variolated, and three years later, she had her daughter undergo variolation. Lady Montagu worked diligently to get the process of variolation accepted by the British.

In a few days, the disease was in full flower. Fortunately, it was usually milder than natural smallpox, so mild that over 90% of the people thus infected survived.

This correspondence and subsequent letters home spurred a series of "**inoculation** parties" in England. In most cases, people did some deep soul-searching before stepping forward for inoculation because they were subjecting themselves to a disease they knew to be horrible. Often, they found comfort in receiving the inoculation with friends and being isolated together while the disease developed. Unfortunately, a small percentage of recipients died in the process.

Nevertheless, the news of inoculation parties spread, and some American colonists gave them a try as well. The first real test of the inoculation method came in 1721, when a smallpox epidemic broke out in Boston. Almost 300 bold Bostonians stepped forward to be inoculated, and only six of the group later contracted smallpox (about 2%). By contrast, the mortality rate among those not inoculated was about 15%.

Variolation Spurs Progress Toward Vaccination

With variolation, the incidence of smallpox began to decline somewhat, especially among the wealthy who could afford the process. Despite the apparent value of this early attempt at inoculation, Cotton Mather and his followers were castigated for interfering with the course of nature. In a series of pamphlets, the opponents of inoculation denounced the practice as sinful and in violation of God's law. To be sure, there was real danger in inoculating oneself with smallpox-tainted pus, but the alternative was almost certain death or disfigurement. Was there any other alternative?

EDWARD JENNER DEVELOPS
A SMALLPOX VACCINE

In the late 1700s, anyone wishing to become a physician had to serve as an apprentice to a physician who had a medical practice. So it was that Edward Jenner, a young man of 13, served his apprenticeship with a surgeon, Daniel Ludlow, in the English countryside. His daily routine brought him in contact with people suffering from various diseases: anthrax, which they acquired from their cows and sheep; tetanus, which developed after a nail or piece of glass penetrated deep into the skin tissues; brucellosis, which caused reproductive organ damage and sterility in cows, pigs, and sheep; and a pattern of high and low fevers in farmers. For some reason, however, the local people did not seem to get smallpox.

Jenner's thoughts stirred, and he inquired why smallpox did not seem to affect those living in the countryside. He was told that farmers, herders, and milkmaids suffered a disease similar to smallpox but much milder. They called it cowpox or **vaccinia** (from *vacca,* the Latin word for "cow"). Cows regularly got cowpox, he was told, and dairy workers sometimes developed mild **lesions** similar to those on the cow's udder. Tradition had it that if you developed cowpox, you would not get smallpox.

Jenner pondered the significance of what he had learned. Could getting cowpox actually protect one against smallpox? Eventually, Jenner finished his apprenticeship and became a physician. Now he was responsible for helping his patients survive smallpox (among other diseases), and he saw the futility of his work. In the back of his mind remained the lessons he had learned years before in the countryside.

Jenner was determined to test his theory that intentionally giving cowpox to people would protect them from smallpox. In May 1796, a dairymaid named Sarah Nelmes came to his office with the lesions of cowpox evident on her hand (Figure 4.2). Jenner asked her to return the next day, when he took some pus from her lesion and injected it superficially into the arm of an eight-year-old boy named James Phipps. The skin developed redness and became sore, but young Phipps did not become ill. Jenner asked him to return several weeks later.

Six weeks later came the experiment that would change the course of medical history. Jenner visited one of his smallpox

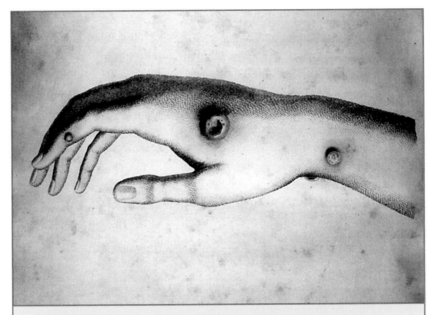

Figure 4.2 This drawing by Edward Jenner shows the hand of Sarah Nelmes, which has obvious lesions of cowpox. Material from these lesions was used to vaccinate James Phipps in 1796.

patients who was very ill and extracted some pus from one of the many lesions on his body. He hurriedly brought the pus back to his office, where he injected it into Phipps's skin. Within three days, Phipps developed a small lesion at the injection site and became feverish. The symptoms did not become any worse, and after 10 days, Phipps was completely well. He had survived injection of virulent smallpox virus. He had been protected by the cowpox.

Jenner was very excited, but he knew that scientists of his day would demand more proof that his method of protection worked. So he continued his experiments for two more years, gradually shifting the source of cowpox pus from an infected person to lesions on the udder of an infected cow. In 1798, he published an historic book describing his method of "vaccination," which documented his method of giving vaccinia (cowpox) to a person to invoke protection against smallpox.

The community is usually skeptical about revolutionary methods of solving health problems, and the climate of 1798 proved to be no exception. Many politicians, clergy, and artists ridiculed the procedure (Figure 4.3). Prominent physicians of the day took sides on the benefit of vaccination versus its risk, and they set out to perform their own experiments. It took no more than a few months for them to be won over. Vaccination was a breakthrough of epic proportions!

Few medical procedures have achieved the instant success of vaccination. By 1801 (three years after Jenner published his book about vaccination), an estimated 100,000 people (worldwide) had been vaccinated. In Paris, Napoleon Bonaparte ordered that his entire army be vaccinated. In Russia, the first child vaccinated was renamed Vaccinor and was educated by the state (at the time, education was a privilege usually only reserved for the wealthy or well-born). In the Americas, President Thomas Jefferson led the effort

EDWARD JENNER

Edward Jenner was a generous, mild-mannered individual with a passion for science. Unlike many physicians of his day, he refused to capitalize on his fame as the "discoverer" of the smallpox vaccine. He vaccinated patients against smallpox for free, unlike many of his colleagues. He weathered much criticism and the attempts of some to discredit him and the originality of his work. He was eventually honored as a fellow of the Royal Society of England, but that honor was bestowed upon him for his work on the nesting habits of the cuckoo bird rather than for his work on smallpox. Throughout his life, Edward Jenner remained a country doctor, spending his entire life in and around the small village of Berkeley, England.

Figure 4.3 Many contemporary politicians, clergy, and artists of Edward Jenner's day ridiculed the idea of using cowpox to prevent disease. In this painting by James Gillray (1757–1815) entitled *Wonderful Effects of the New Inoculation*, notice the cows and cow parts "sprouting" from the various recipients of the vaccine.

to have as many people vaccinated as possible. In a letter to Jenner, Jefferson wrote,

> You have erased from the calendar of human affliction one of its greatest. Yours is the comfortable reflection that mankind will never forget that you have lived.

Within 10 years of Jenner's inoculation of James Phipps, the entire world had accepted the practice of vaccination.

THE IMPLICATIONS OF VACCINATION

Vaccination was the first-ever attempt to control disease on an international scale and, as such, it has been hailed as one of the

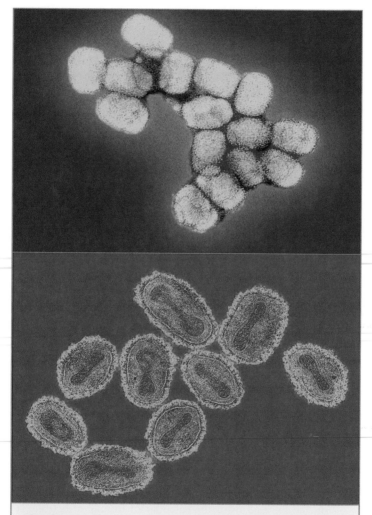

Figure 4.4 These electron micrographs show vaccinia (top) and variola (bottom) viruses. Morphologically, the viruses are very similar and are almost indistinguishable when viewed with the electron microscope. They are stained differently in these micrographs.

great medical and social advances of history. Essentially, it protected the community as well as the individual, and so it represented one of the first attempts at public health. On a philosophical level, it showed that an infectious disease could be controlled, something no one had dared think possible before vaccination was developed.

The use of vaccination preceded by over 100 years an understanding of how vaccination works. Today's scientists know that cowpox and smallpox viruses are very similar to one another (Figure 4.4). Both are rectangular in shape and about the same size, and the genetic material (**DNA**) of both is similar (but not exactly the same).

When cowpox virus enters the body, the immune system produces proteins called **antibodies** that react with and neutralize the cowpox virus. There is also an added bonus: The antibodies react with and neutralize the smallpox virus should it appear in the future. Thus, the body acquires immunity to the cowpox virus and, also very importantly, to the smallpox virus. (See Chapter 5 for a more detailed discussion of the smallpox virus.)

It is almost impossible to discuss smallpox without mentioning vaccination. As mentioned earlier, vaccination was largely responsible for the eradication of smallpox from the world. However, as described in Chapter 7, there remains the risk that the smallpox virus may be used as a weapon by bioterrorists. Immunizing a population by vaccination is a prime deterrent to bioterrorism (Chapter 9) and vaccination is essential to stem the spread of the disease. In few places in medical history has a process like vaccination had such a profound impact.

5

The Smallpox Virus

Viruses are among the tiniest **microbes** known to exist. The larger viruses are about the same size as a small **bacterium**, while the smaller viruses are about the same size as a **ribosome**, the ultramicroscopic cell structure where proteins are formed. To appreciate the small size of a virus, consider that 500 "typical" viruses could fit inside a single bacterium of average dimensions. An ordinary light microscope is generally useless when trying to see a virus; instead, a highly sophisticated electron microscope must be used.

Despite their incredibly small size, viruses can infect and destroy **cells** thousands of times larger than themselves. They accomplish this by invading the host cells and releasing their genes within the cells. The cells then become chemical factories for producing hundreds of new viruses. In this ultimate example of **parasitism**, the virus uses the cell's components to reproduce itself in a process known as **replication**. At replication's end, the new viruses leave behind a severely damaged, often dead, host cell. As this wave of cell damage and death spreads, infection and disease follow.

THE COMPOSITION OF A VIRUS

Viruses are exceptions to the general view that microbial cells (such as bacteria and protozoa) cause human disease. This is because viruses are not cells. They have no **cytoplasm**, no **nucleus**, and no cellular structures such as **mitochondria**, **Golgi bodies**, ribosomes, or **lysosomes**. Rather, viruses are composed of nothing more than a molecule of DNA or **RNA** enclosed in protein. (The eminent 1960 Nobel laureate Peter Medawar had described a virus as "a piece of bad news wrapped in

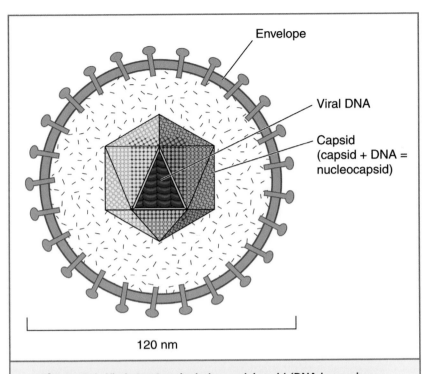

Envelope

Viral DNA

Capsid
(capsid + DNA =
nucleocapsid)

120 nm

Figure 5.1 Viral structure includes nucleic acid (DNA in poxviruses such as smallpox) surrounded by a protein coat called the capsid. The nucleic acid plus capsid is called the nucleocapsid. In some viruses, the nucleocapsid makes up the virion. In enveloped viruses, the nucleocapsid is surrounded by a lipoprotein envelope. The virion of an enveloped virus is composed of the nucleic acid, the capsid, and the envelope.

protein.") The DNA or RNA molecule of the virus is called its **genome**, while the protein wrapping is known as its **capsid** (kap' sid). In some viruses, a surrounding membrane called an **envelope** encloses the capsid. A complex viral particle is often referred to as a **virion** (vī'-rē-on). See Figure 5.1 for a schematic of viral structure.

The capsid of the virus is usually responsible for the shape of a virus. In some viruses, such as those that cause colds (adenoviruses), the capsid assumes a shape resembling a soccer ball, a geometric figure composed of 20 triangular faces. This figure is known as an **icosahedron** (i-kos-ah-HE-dron), and the virus possessing this shape is said to have icosahedral symmetry. Other virus capsids take the shape of a tightly coiled spiral, called a helix. These viruses, such as the rabies virus, have helical symmetry. Viruses that are neither icosahedral nor helical are said to have complex symmetry (Figure 5.2). The smallpox virus is an example of a virus with complex symmetry.

The smallpox virus, a member of the *Poxviridae* **family** and the *orthopoxvirus* **genus**, has a genome composed of DNA (the largest of all viral genomes) and an elaborate capsid with an enclosing envelope. The capsid is rectangular and resembles a brick, with the proteins of the capsid organized into a series of rod-like structures. The smallpox virus is comparatively large, measuring about 0.400 micrometer (μm) in length and about 0.20 μm in width and depth. Because of the large size and distinctive shape of the virus, diseases caused by poxviruses are easily diagnosed by direct examination of tissues using electron microscopy.

The envelope of the smallpox virus is very similar to the membrane of a typical cell, except that it contains proteins associated only with smallpox viruses. The virus does not synthesize this envelope in the same way that cells synthesize their cell membranes. Rather, the smallpox virus acquires its envelope at the end of its replication cycle when a genome enclosed in its capsid, the **nucleocapsid**, forces its way through the cell membrane and wraps itself in a piece of the membrane.

Alternatively, the viruses may remain in the cell without acquiring envelopes. These non-enveloped viruses are released from the cell when it dies. Although non-enveloped, they are still infectious.

Having an envelope does have its advantages. It helps the smallpox virus evade body defenses because envelopes do not spark the same immune responses as non-enveloped

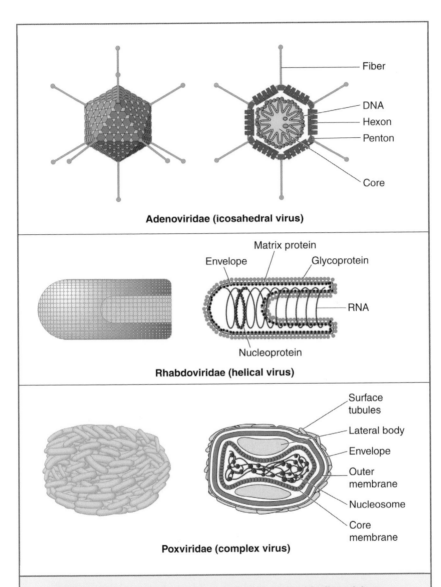

Figure 5.2 Icosahedral viruses (adenovirus in this figure) have their capsids organized into geometric patterns with cubic symmetry. Helical viruses have a capsid that winds into a helix. These viruses are represented in the figure by the rhabdovirus (rabies). Complex viruses have no common organization patterns. The smallpox virus is a complex virus.

nucleocapsids. Also, the viral proteins in the envelope help the smallpox virus locate its next host cell for replication, as we shall see next.

VIRAL REPLICATION

The replication process for viruses is unlike anything known to occur elsewhere in the world of nature. In simple terms, a virus takes over a cell and uses it for its own purposes to form new viruses. The cell destruction occurring at the end of the process helps explain virtually all viral diseases.

In order to replicate, a virus must locate a particular type of host cell capable of supporting the process. Polioviruses, for example, replicate primarily in cells of the nervous system, while hepatitis viruses require liver cells for their replication.

For the smallpox virus, the major hosts are cells in the skin's **epidermis**, although other body cells can support replication of poxviruses. Knowing which cells a virus uses gives us a clue as to how the virus is transmitted and where symptoms occur. Since the smallpox virus exists in skin tissue, we can anticipate that the symptoms of smallpox will occur on the skin, and indeed the smallpox rash is the hallmark of the disease.

Upon reaching their target cells, viruses must gain access to the cells' cytoplasm. For some viruses, the cell performs **phagocytosis** and engulfs the viruses along with particles of food or droplets of fluid. In other cases, a virus attaches to the surface of the cell and biochemically dissolves the cell membrane, thereby providing an entryway into the cytoplasm. Enveloped viruses, such as smallpox, use their envelopes to gain penetration: First, the virus binds its envelope protein with a highly specific docking site on the cell membrane called a receptor, and then, the viral envelope blends with the cell membrane (much like combining olive oil and corn oil) and the nucleocapsid slips into the cell interior. Figure 5.3 illustrates this process.

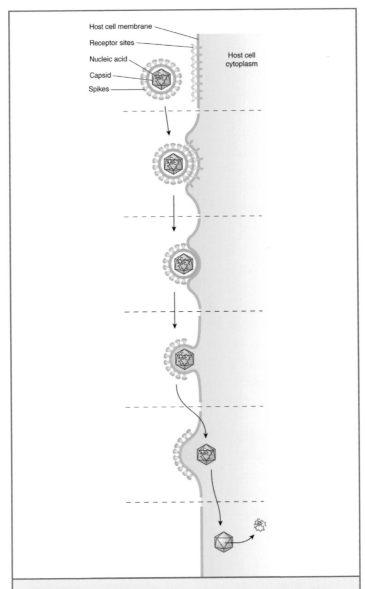

Host cell membrane
Receptor sites
Nucleic acid
Capsid
Spikes
Host cell
cytoplasm

Figure 5.3 Enveloped viruses, such as the smallpox virus, enter the host cell by fusing their viral envelope with the cell membrane of the target cell. Following fusion, the nucleocapsid enters the cytoplasm of the host cell, where the virus will begin the process of replication.

Once within the cell cytoplasm, the nucleocapsid uses cell **enzymes** to dissolve its capsid, thereby freeing the DNA. The DNA consists of a set of genes that encodes the enzymes necessary to synthesize RNA and new DNA for new smallpox viruses. The genes also encode proteins that make up the new capsids for new viruses. And finally, some of the genes encode proteins that dot the viral envelope to ensure union of smallpox virus with its next host cell. DNA replication, as well as the assembly of new smallpox viruses, takes place in the host cell cytoplasm (see the box below).

Even though the smallpox virus contains proteins to assist its own replication, it still must rely on the host cell to provide many of the replication components needed before new virions can be assembled. For instance, it has no **amino acids** of its own for making proteins, so it must rely on the host cell to provide them. It has no nucleotides for synthesizing new DNA, so it relies on the cell's supply. Any compounds that supply energy to the chemical reactions must come from the cell. It also has no ribosomes, the workbenches where proteins are synthesized, so these must be supplied by the cell. In short, virtually all the cell's resources are redirected toward replicating the virus.

SMALLPOX VIRUS REPLICATION

Unlike most DNA-containing viruses that must migrate to the host cell's nucleus to begin replication, the smallpox virus completes its entire replication cycle in the host cell cytoplasm. This can be accomplished because the pox virus particle contains a viral **RNA polymerase**, which begins transcription of the viral DNA into **messenger RNA** immediately following host cell entry. In addition to RNA polymerase, many other proteins are present in the viral core, providing the virus with its own transcription system. Consequently, there is no need to migrate to the nucleus of the host cell to utilize the transcriptional machinery found there.

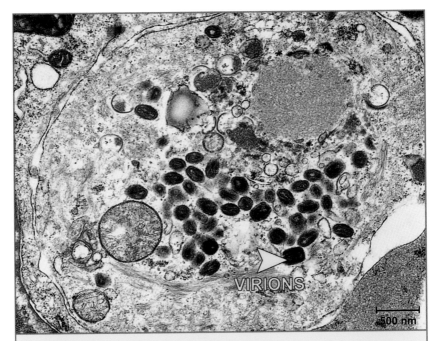

Figure 5.4 Smallpox virions (labeled here) accumulate in the host cell cytoplasm following replication. Each virus is approximately 0.4 μm by 0.2 μm (1000 nm = 1 μm).

After approximately six hours, new nucleocapsids begin to appear in the cell cytoplasm, as shown in Figure 5.4. Now some of the nucleocapsids begin to migrate toward the cell membrane. On reaching the membrane, they force their way through and enclose themselves in bits of membranes studded with viral proteins. This process, called **budding**, results in hundreds of new, enveloped smallpox viruses.

Budding also has a devastating effect on the host cell because the process leaves gaping holes in the membrane that the cell cannot repair quickly enough, so it leaks to death. Also recall that the cell has lost the bulk of its essential nutrients and energy compounds to viral replication and, chemically speaking, it is in dire straits. Soon the cell will probably die and disintegrate.

But this is not the end of the host's problems, for the cell may have released 500 or more poxviruses into the immediate vicinity. These viruses will easily locate new host cells by random collisions, and infection of a new host cell will yield 500 more poxviruses. (Consider that 500 viruses replicating in 500 cells will yield 250,000 viruses. If 250,000 viruses attack 250,000 cells, the problem of viral infection grows serious very quickly). As these host cells die, the number of viruses rises geometrically and the infection spreads. Soon, the tell-tale skin lesions of smallpox appear. The disease is well on its way to causing the devastating symptoms of smallpox, as discussed in the next chapter.

CULTIVATING VIRUSES

It should be clear from the discussions that follow that viruses cannot be cultivated in the **agar media** used for bacteria, fungi, and other microbes. Rather, since viruses use living cells for replication, the cultivation methods for viruses tend to be complex. Scientists need large quantities of viruses for research purposes and for use in vaccines, so they have developed methods for growing the viruses outside of the body.

Cultivating Viruses in a Fertilized Chicken Egg

Among the first viral cultivation methods was the fertilized chicken egg described as early as 1931 by Alice Woodruff and Ernest Goodpasture. This method, which is still used for cultivating poxviruses, requires inoculation of the virus into the chorioallantoic (kôr'-ē-ō-al-əntō'-ik) membrane, or CAM, of the egg (Figure 5.5). The process must be conducted under carefully controlled conditions to limit fungal and bacterial contamination.

The Tissue Culture Method

During the 1950s, scientists developed the second major method of viral cultivation, the tissue culture method. The

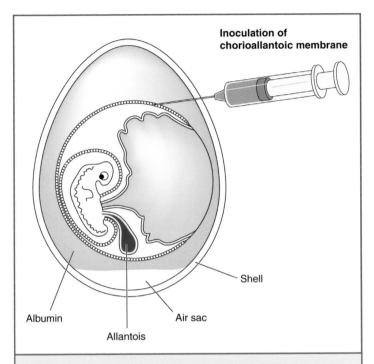

Inoculation of
chorioallantoic membrane

Shell

Albumin

Air sac

Allantois

Figure 5.5 Poxviruses may be grown in an embryonating chicken egg by inoculating the chorioallantoic membrane (CAM) of the egg. The CAM is the outermost membrane in the egg that surrounds the chicken embryo. Poxviruses will grow on the membrane and produce characteristic pocks.

breakthrough in this development was the finding that an enzyme called trypsin could free cells from their surrounding tissue without damaging the cells. When the cells are placed in a nutrient-rich fluid in tubes or Petri dishes, they attach to the surface of the vessel. Then they multiply and spread to form a sheet of cells one cell thick, a so-called monolayer. When viruses are inoculated to the monolayers, the number of viruses increases dramatically.

The tissue culture technique had a profound effect on the study of viruses because it made huge quantities of viruses available for research. It also had a considerable public health benefit because enough viruses could now be grown to prepare vaccines.

Since its inception, the tissue culture method and its variations have become the basis for many studies of viruses. In some cases, the tissue cells came directly from animals; these are called **primary cell cultures** (in rare cases, the animals themselves are used to cultivate the viruses). In other cases, one type of cell from the primary cell culture is taken and cultured apart from other cells to obtain a set of genetically identical cells. These cells can be passed, or subcultured, up to approximately 50 times. These types of cell lines, called **secondary diploid cell lines**, make it easier to study the effects of the virus on its host cells.

WHAT IS THE SMALLPOX GENOME?

Determining the exact sequence of all the **nucleotides** contained within the genetic material of a virus provides us with the genetic blueprint of that virus. This information may then be used to compare genetic information of one virus to another, identify genes and determine their functions, and perhaps most importantly, identify target genes involved in disease processes. Scientists can then either inactivate or use the genes to produce a DNA-based vaccine to protect the host from the disease process.

In 1991, Joe Esposito and Craig Venter sequenced the Rahima strain of variola. The virus was found to have a genome of 186 **kilobases** encoding for approximately 187 genes. Since those initial sequencing efforts, several more strains of variola virus and vaccinia virus have been sequenced. VECTOR Laboratory (a Russian company) sequenced nine strains of variola major virus and one of variola minor virus. Information from the sequencing efforts suggests that poxviruses have genomes in the range of 165 to 210 kilobases, with gene sequences for structural, membrane, and core proteins highly conserved among members of the viral family. The approximate

5% difference among pox genomes probably accounts for differences in infectivity, lethality, and host range.

Armed with the knowledge of the genetic sequence of several strains of variola virus, researchers have now identified several poxvirus genes that resemble mammalian proteins, including those that inhibit host defenses. These genes include DNA-encoding **interferon** receptors, **cytokine** receptors, and a complement binding protein (see Chapters 6 and 7 for a more detailed description of interferons, cytokines, and complement binding proteins). Perhaps the presence of these genes allows enhanced viral replication by circumventing host cell protective responses. Ongoing research on the poxvirus genome will hopefully yield new clues about the virus's host range and virulence, allowing us to develop better vaccines and new therapies in the (hopefully) unlikely event that the virus should reemerge or be maliciously released somewhere in the world.

6

Smallpox: The Disease

Until it was eradicated in 1977, smallpox was among the most horrible and gruesome diseases known to science. The smallpox virus had a deep affinity for human beings, and some historians contend that smallpox killed more people than any other disease, including the dreaded Black Death of the 1300s. The disease was accompanied by pus-filled skin lesions, called **pustules**, that encased the body and made it look like a cobblestone street. The pain and suffering were extraordinary, and survival from the disease was uncertain.

THE BEGINNING OF SMALLPOX

Before 1977, smallpox was a contagious disease, most often spread through the respiratory route. The virus could be found in the pus of the lesions that developed in the mouth and nose, as well as the lesions that covered the patient's skin. Transmission of the virus through the air when the patient coughed, sneezed, or simply talked to people close by occurred easily.

Moreover, the virus remained active in the lesions on the skin and was available for transmission throughout the duration of the disease or even after the patient died. The clothing and bedding of the patient were potential sources of virus as well. However, this was a less likely source of infection because viruses that are enclosed in hard, dried scabs (which are heavy and not usually inhaled) are not as infectious as those from oral secretions.

Smallpox has an incubation period of 7 to 17 days, with an average of 12 days. During this time, the virus, which probably entered the patient through the nose or mouth by either inhalation or contact with infected fingers, begins to multiply. The virus then disseminates through the body via the **lymph** and blood. At this point in the infection process, few symptoms of disease are apparent, and patients generally feel well. In addition, no virus is yet being shed by the patient, so transmission of the disease normally does not occur during this period.

Once the incubation period is complete, symptoms of the disease are evidenced by a sharp rise in fever accompanied by backache and vomiting. The virus, which has localized in the small blood vessels of the skin, begins to replicate rapidly, causing lesions.

These lesions initially develop in the mouth, where they quickly begin to release considerable amounts of smallpox virus into the saliva. When the patient talks or coughs, millions of viruses are released into the air in tiny droplets of mucus and saliva, and nearby people inhaling these droplets can be infected.

In addition, patients also experience severe fatigue and physical collapse (known as prostration), and consequently become bedridden. Because these symptoms could reflect numerous diseases, however, there is little evidence that the disease is smallpox. The unique rash that follows identifies smallpox for what it is.

SMALLPOX TAKES ITS TOLL

As noted above, the first signs of the smallpox rash occur as lesions in the mouth. Then the rash spreads to the face, forearms, trunk, and legs. Initially, the rash presents itself as tiny pink to red spots called **macules** (mak'-yŏŏlz). The macules are densest on the palms of the hands and soles of the feet, as well as on the face, arms, and legs (Figure 6.1). The distribution of smallpox lesions is considered a helpful diagnostic tool.

Macules develop into pink pimples called **papules**

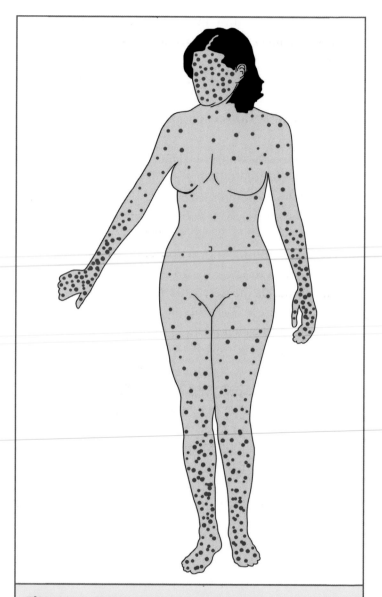

Figure 6.1 The distribution of smallpox rash over the body is fairly diagnostic for disease. Lesions are most numerous on the face and limbs (especially the palms of the hands and soles of the feet). Because all lesions mature at the same rate, the rash of smallpox is often described as synchronous.

(pap'-yōōlz), which grow into small, raised bumps called **vesicles** (ves'-ik-əlz). Within two to three days, the vesicles swell with pus, and take on a new name: pustules.

The blister-like pustules are extremely painful, and as they expand and accumulate pus, the pressure results in an intense burning sensation in the skin. Death, if it occurs, will often happen at this point in the disease. However, if the patient survives the attack, the fluid in the lesions will begin to be absorbed and the lesions will flatten. By the end of the second week of the rash, the lesions crust over and scabs develop. The scabs eventually fall off, leaving areas of scarred, depigmented skin described as a pock. Deep pitting and scarring result when the sebaceous glands of the skin are severely affected by the virus. Because sebaceous glands are most numerous on the face, this is where pockmarks are most numerous (Figure 6.2).

During past generations, physicians estimated that during outbreaks of ordinary smallpox, about 30% of unvaccinated individuals died and 70% lived. Why or how does death occur? Unfortunately, when smallpox existed in nature, outbreaks occurred in countries or regions where it was difficult to carry out pathological studies; therefore, the precise cause of death from smallpox was not well documented. Due to successful eradication efforts, we now have no way to determine the exact cause(s) of death in humans from this disease, so we must rely on animal models such as mousepox or monkeypox to provide some clues.

These models and limited information from outbreaks in the 1960s and 1970s suggest that death may be the result of either viral **toxemia** or the accumulation of circulating immune complexes composed of antibody and **antigen** that are not sufficiently cleared from the body. In some cases, complications such as encephalitis (inflammation of the brain) were the cause of death.

Figure 6.2 As a result of smallpox infection, the skin is often left with pockmarks. The largest concentration of pockmarks is usually on the face, due to the large number of sebaceous glands found there.

TYPES OF SMALLPOX
Variola Major

The disease we have been describing so far in this book is the classic form of smallpox known as variola major. Variola major, or ordinary smallpox, was prevalent in Asia, parts of Africa, and Europe.

Flat-Type Smallpox

Most cases of variola major developed as we have explained above, but, in some instances, a flat-type smallpox occurred. Here, the skin lesions, which were flat rather than raised, developed more slowly (or not at all), but damage to the internal organs was much more severe, and fever remained high throughout the course of the disease. Flat-type smallpox is also called malignant smallpox because more people ended up dying from this disease than from ordinary smallpox.

Hemorrhagic-Type Smallpox

Other types of smallpox caused hemorrhaging from many sites on the body (hemorrhagic-type smallpox), including the skin, **conjunctiva**, and **mucous membranes**. Hemorrhagic-type smallpox most often occurred in adults and frequently caused death due to heart failure. In one type of hemorrhagic smallpox, the skin would become dark purple due to **subcutaneous** bleeding. This form of variola major was called black pox. Both flat-type and hemorrhagic-type smallpox were very lethal, causing death in approximately 96% of patients.

Variola Minor

A less deadly form of smallpox is called variola minor, or alastrim (al' astrim). Variola minor was evident in the United States, Europe, South America, and Africa in the late 1800s to mid-1900s. The virus causing variola minor is genetically distinct from the variola major virus and is thought to have arisen in southern Africa and the West Indies. Variola minor infection caused a milder form of smallpox, with very low mortality among patients (only about 1% of patients died). The pustules were smaller, and damage to the internal organs was minimal. The patient often remained active and mobile during infection. Following recovery, the patient became pockmarked, although not as severely as those with variola major.

HOW THE BODY RESPONDS WHEN INFECTED WITH SMALLPOX

The large, complex smallpox virus usually stimulates a rigorous **immune response** in the patient (see the Immunology Primer

IMMUNOLOGY PRIMER

Immunity: A state of protection or resistance to a specific pathogen.

B lymphocyte or **B cell**: Lymphocyte that matures in the bone marrow and other lymphoid tissue. B cells differentiate into plasma cells, which produce protective proteins called antibodies.

Antibody: Protective proteins produced in response to a specific antigen (anything considered "nonself"). An antibody combines with that specific antigen to produce an antibody/antigen complex.

Complement: A series of 20 serum proteins that, once activated by an antibody/antigen complex, form a cascade that ultimately results in the destruction of viral-infected cells.

Immune complexes: Antigen and antibody complexes (precipitates or agglutinates) that are usually cleared from the body by phagocytic cells.

Phagocytic cells: "Eating" cells such as neutrophils and macrophages responsible for removing (and killing, if necessary) organisms and debris from the body.

T lymphocyte or **T cell**: A thymus-derived lymphocyte that functions in the **cell-mediated arm** of the immune response. T cells may function as killers (**cytotoxic T cells**), or produce various cytokines, which influence the activity of other cells.

Cytokines: Small proteins produced by one cell, often T cells and macrophages, that influence other cells, especially T cells. Some examples of cytokines include interferons and interleukins.

Memory: The second and each subsequent time the host is exposed to a specific antigen, the immune response will be more rapid and intensified due to the presence of memory cells that are primed and ready to respond to that antigen.

Antigen (adv. **antigenically**): Cell or viral components that induce a specific host immune response.

box on Page 62 for definitions of immunology terms). In response to smallpox infection, host **B cells** produce antibody, which functions to:

- Bind to viruses and prevent them from attaching to host cells,

- Bind to **complement** to **lyse** viruses, and

- Form **immune complexes**, which can then be easily cleared by the body's phagocytic cells.

Our knowledge of the **cell-mediated arm** of the immune system and our understanding of the complex function of **T cells** has virtually exploded in the last 30 years. Unfortunately, this information comes a little too late to determine exactly how this important branch of the immune response functions in humans when infected with smallpox virus.

An attack of smallpox results in life-long immunity to the disease, indicating that **memory** functions of both B and T cells are robust as a result of disease. Because poxviruses are so similar **antigenically**, infection with one (vaccinia virus) results in protective immunity against the other (variola virus).

7

Treating Smallpox

When antibiotics came into widespread use in the 1940s and 1950s, they were hailed as miracle drugs. For example, bacterial pneumonia was generally regarded as a terminal disease before that time, but with penicillin therapy, patients made great strides and soon recovered. Similarly, dreaded diseases such as typhoid fever, syphilis, tuberculosis, and cholera soon came under control.

However, scientists and physicians were dismayed to learn that viruses were not susceptible to the new antibiotics. Polio, hepatitis, rabies, influenza, and many other viral diseases, including smallpox, continued to spread waves of fear as they swept through populations unchecked.

Researchers soon learned why the antibiotics were ineffective: Viruses simply did not do anything that antibiotics could interfere with. Penicillin, for instance, reacts with the cell walls of bacteria, and viruses have no cell walls. Tetracycline, another antibiotic, interferes with the synthesis of protein in bacterial cytoplasm, and viruses have no protein synthesis going on beneath their capsids. Sulfa drugs bring to a halt certain biochemical pathways in bacteria, pathways that do not exist in viruses.

Thus, through the first 50 years of the antibiotic age, viruses remained exempt from the "antibiotic effect." Therefore, instead of *treating* viral diseases, scientists turned their attention to methods for *preventing* viral diseases. Eventually, that effort led to viral vaccines: vaccines that do not cause infection in the body, but stimulate its immune system to produce protein antibodies. The antibodies circulate in the blood much like a protective army programmed to react with and neutralize a single enemy. The polio vaccine, for example, elicits polio antibodies that will unite with and destroy polioviruses, and only polioviruses.

VIRAL VACCINES

Early successes with viral vaccines made headlines in the 1950s with the Salk and Sabin vaccines for polio. The Salk injectable vaccine uses chemically treated polioviruses whose nucleic acid molecules have been destroyed, while the Sabin oral vaccine employs slow-replicating viruses whose nucleic acid molecules are intact.

By the 1960s, vaccines were available for measles, mumps, and rubella (the MMR preparation). During the succeeding decades, scientists developed vaccines for hepatitis A, hepatitis B, influenza, chicken pox, yellow fever, and other viral diseases. So, while the public health approach to bacterial disease was treatment, the public health approach to viral disease was prevention.

The Smallpox Vaccine

Through all these years of vaccine research, the smallpox vaccine stood as a model for what could be accomplished through prevention. The extraordinary effort to eradicate smallpox and its outstanding success were the hallmarks of public health at its best. Nowhere was vaccine put to a greater test and nowhere did it better address the challenge.

And well it did, for smallpox is a deadly disease that defies treatment. Once a person developed the fearsome symptoms of smallpox, there was little that could be done, except to make the person as comfortable as possible. If patients recovered, they had only their immune systems to thank, because no type of medical intervention halted the destruction of the disease.

The patient's antibodies interact with the envelope and capsid of the smallpox virus and prevent the virus from uniting with its host cell. Surrounded by antibodies in the bloodstream, the virus is an easy target for the body's white blood cells. These cells digest the antibody-enshrouded virus in a process called phagocytosis. Unfortunately, this process does not occur vigorously enough in many patients, and the smallpox viruses caused death in about 30% of their victims.

But suppose a vaccine was used immediately after a person was exposed to smallpox viruses? Could the body produce enough antibodies in time to surround and destroy the virus before it caused too much damage to the patient's system? The answer apparently is yes, although more research is needed to provide a more definite answer. Scientists believe that if a smallpox vaccine were administered within four days of the exposure, this would be enough time for the body's immune system to produce sufficient antibodies to protect the body from damage. The idea is to mount an immune response before the virus has replicated to such an extent that the body systems can no longer function well.

Strictly speaking, a vaccine used after an individual has been exposed is more precaution than treatment, but this is a matter of semantics. The essential criterion is that a person is in real danger of becoming seriously ill within days, and that person is being *treated* with the vaccine to *prevent* the illness.

CURRENT VACCINE STRATEGIES

Although the last known case of smallpox in the United States occurred in 1949, production in the United States of smallpox vaccine continued until 1975. In 1971, the United States Public Health Service terminated its smallpox vaccination program, and, in 1982, the WHO deleted smallpox from travel vaccine requirements. Routine vaccination ceased in all countries of the world in 1986, with Israel being the only country that routinely continues to vaccinate its military personnel to the present.

Preparing the Vaccine

In the past, live vaccinia (strain *Lister elstree*) virus was injected into calves or sheep. The pocks that developed on the animal's skin were then scraped, and **phenol** was added to the preparation to kill contaminating bacteria but not the virus. The suspension was then freeze-dried and resuspended in sterile **buffer**. The vaccine strain used was held by the WHO in Bilthoven, Netherlands, to ensure uniform preparation of vaccine world-wide. Vaccines prepared in this way are stored for 18 years, after which time they are still potent.

Currently, several new strains of the virus are being used to produce new vaccines. These include a modified non-replicating vaccinia strain (*Vaccinia ankara*), and a vaccinia strain (*Lister*) grown in tissue culture (Chapter 5) rather than on the skin of live animals.

As genetic techniques have become more routine in their use, we have learned through genetic analysis that the vaccine strains used are not actually cowpox (vaccinia), but rather what appears to be a (variola) smallpox-cowpox-horsepox hybrid. Where, when, or how this change/mutation or hybridization occurred is unknown.

Vaccination Details

To vaccinate an individual, the skin is first cleaned with water. No rubbing alcohol should be used because it can kill the virus in the vaccine. A sterile, disposable, bifurcated needle (Figure 7.1) is then dipped into rehydrated vaccine, and is applied to the skin by poking a 5-mm zone on the deltoid muscle of the upper arm 15 times with the needle (Figure 7.2). If done correctly, a trace of blood should appear. A loose gauze dressing should be applied to the vaccine site. A pimple or papule appears after 3 to 4 days. The papule eventually increases in size, scabs over in two weeks (Figure 7.3), falls off, and leaves a pink scar that can be seen on the upper arm of almost everyone currently over the age of 35.

Vaccine protection lasts approximately 10 years, with current research suggesting that even after 10 years, symptoms and death rates from smallpox infection in vaccinated people will be much less severe than in those who never were vaccinated.

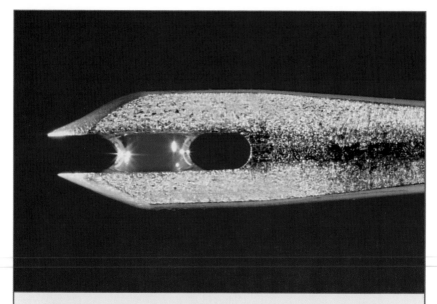

Figure 7.1 Bifurcated needles (shown here) played a role in the success of the smallpox eradication program. They were cheap ($5 per 1,000), could be sterilized for reuse, and held a specific amount of vaccine (0.0025 ml). Also, a local villager could be trained to vaccinate using the needle in 10 to 15 minutes.

The current smallpox vaccine is not recommended for any individual who is:

- Human immunodeficiency virus (HIV)-positive,

- Immunosuppressed,

- Pregnant, or

- Has a history of **eczema**.

Vaccine complications, although rare, range from mild to severe and generally fall into one of four major recognized categories: eczema vaccinatum, progressive vaccinia, generalized vaccinia, and post-vaccinial encephalitis. Table 7.1 provides a clinical description of the four complications.

COMPLICATION	CLINICAL MANIFESTATION
Eczema Vaccinatum	Severely inflamed lesions erupting on the skin in any areas where eczema was present. Also high fever and swollen lymph nodes. Mortality high.
Progressive Vaccinia	Vaccine lesion fails to heal. Additional lesions spread progressively over the skin. Patient usually dies in 2 to 5 months.
Generalized Vaccinia	Rash covers the whole body as a result of vaccination. Prognosis good.
Post-vaccinial Encephalitis	Central nervous system inflammation often resulting in death.

Table 7.1 Complications of Smallpox Vaccination in Susceptible Individuals

Eczema vaccinatum usually occurs in individuals with a history of eczema, which is why vaccination for them is not recommended. Progressive vaccinia occurs in those who are immunosuppressed. Generalized vaccinia and post-vaccinial encephalitis are sometimes seen in otherwise healthy individuals. Vaccinia immunoglobulin (VIG), or prepared antibody against the virus, may be used to treat encephalitis, the most deadly of all the complications.

With the United States' renewal vaccination program in 2003, in which 475,000 individuals (40,000 civilians, the rest military) were vaccinated, 39 cases of generalized vaccinia, 1 case of encephalitis, and 0 cases of eczema vaccinatum and progressive vaccinia were reported.

The good news is that the complication rate seems to be low; however, the bad news is that we are seeing new complications

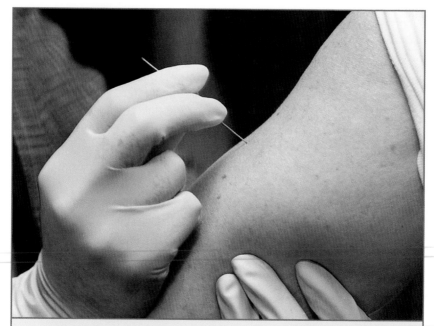

Figure 7.2 Using a bifurcated needle, the smallpox vaccine is administered to the upper arm using 15 strokes to deliver the virus.

of vaccination that have not been seen in the past. The new complications include effects on the cardiovascular system, particularly myopericarditis (inflammation of the muscle and membrane surrounding the heart) and ischemia (poor blood flow to the heart). Why these new complications? Scientists believe that complications observed now but not in the past are due to the fact that in the past we vaccinated mostly children, whereas now we are vaccinating adults. Unlike children, adults often have known or unknown chronic disease, making it more likely that they will develop vaccine complications.

While stockpiles of vaccine are now at desired levels, there is currently a shortage of the bifurcated needles needed for vaccination and a shortage of VIG needed to treat vaccine side effects. Given the recent progress with stockpiling vaccine and supplies and research to develop a safer, more reliable

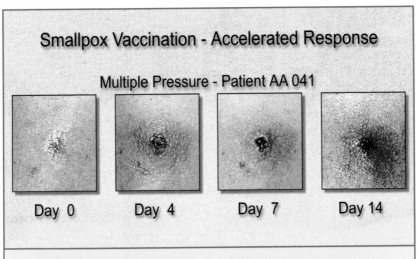

Figure 7.3 Following smallpox vaccination, the site progresses through a series of lesions. This progression represents a "take," or successful vaccination effort resulting in immunity to smallpox virus for approximately the next 10 years.

vaccine, the questions about and controversy surrounding the smallpox vaccine still remain. Is the risk of adverse side effects high enough to warrant vaccination for a disease or virus that, as far as we know, no longer exists in the world outside of two secure laboratories? The question of the smallpox threat will be discussed in Chapter 9.

While the pros and cons of reinstituting a smallpox vaccination program continue to be debated, other scientists have concentrated their efforts on developing a smallpox treatment. We shall examine the fruits of their efforts next.

DRUGS DEVELOPED TO TREAT SMALLPOX

Until the close of the 20th century, physicians had very few antiviral agents at their disposal. One reason was the lack of targets, since viruses have a simple structure and virtually no ongoing chemical processes. Scientists, therefore, focused on the replication process and sought to interrupt it.

Their work was rewarded in the 1980s with discovery of the drug amantadine. Amantadine (available as Symmetrel®) binds to influenza viruses and prevents them from attaching to their host cells in the respiratory tract. A new drug named oseltamivir (Tamiflu®) performs the same activity. Those with AIDS often take azidothymidine (AZT), a drug that interferes with the action of HIV genes in the cytoplasm of host cells. Part of the anti-AIDS regime generally includes a protease inhibitor (such as ritonavir or Crixivan®), which interferes with synthesis of viral capsids.

Cidofovir

One of the newer antiviral drugs in development is cidofovir. Cidofovir was synthesized by Belgian chemists in 1993. When tested against a variety of viruses, cidofovir was found to be active against cowpox (vaccinia) viruses cultivated in tissue culture. Cidofovir, which works by inhibiting an enzyme necessary for the virus to reproduce, proved equally effective in animal studies.

Next, scientists tested the drug against the smallpox virus. In 1995, laboratory tests were performed in the United States in animals inoculated with smallpox virus. The tests were carried out in the highest security laboratory at the U.S. Army installation at Fort Detrick, Maryland. The results indicated that cidofovir is active against 31 strains of smallpox virus as well as numerous strains of the closely related monkeypox virus.

Of course, treating animals in a high-security research laboratory is a far cry from treating people during an epidemic when tension and emotions are high. Nevertheless, the tests support the possibility that cidofovir could be used against smallpox, especially if a vaccine is also used. One major drawback to cidofovir's use is that the drug must be injected intravenously to be effective. Another is that toxic side effects cannot be adequately assessed in ill patients because no one has had smallpox in a quarter-century.

Interferon

A report sponsored by the American Society for Microbiology at the 2003 Biodefense Research Meeting suggests that interferon may be useful as a treatment for smallpox infection. Interferons are antiviral proteins produced by the cell in response to viral infection. These nonspecific cytokines will protect adjacent cells from viral infection. Although it is not possible to test the efficacy of interferon in humans against the smallpox or variola virus, we can study its effects in mice. Mice infected with the cowpox virus received interferon through their noses. Those mice receiving interferon had a 95% survival rate, while the virus was deadly in those mice that received no interferon. Though the results are impressive, again, the difficulty with this work is proving that the drug provides the same degree of protection for humans as it does for mice.

8

Should the Smallpox Virus Be Destroyed?

On August 11, 1978, a 40-year-old medical photographer named Janet Parker was working in the anatomy department on the floor above the smallpox laboratory at the University of Birmingham Medical School in England. She was feeling feverish. Unbeknownst to her, smallpox virus had wafted up from the laboratory below 12 days earlier, and now the virus was replicating in the tissues of her body. By August 15, a rash appeared on her skin and, by August 25, she was in the throes of smallpox.

The medical establishment worked quickly to vaccinate and quarantine close to 300 people who had been in contact with Parker. Of that group, only her mother developed smallpox. She survived, but her daughter Janet did not.

Under other circumstances, this outbreak of smallpox might not have received any special attention. However, what makes this outbreak unique is the date of its occurrence—1978, almost a full year after the last case of smallpox occurred in nature. The incident is offered as evidence of what can happen when the last stocks of smallpox virus are saved, even in closely controlled environments. But we are getting ahead of ourselves. To understand the debate about whether to save samples of the smallpox virus, we must first examine more closely how smallpox was eradicated.

THE END OF SMALLPOX

October 26, 1977, was a momentous day in the history of smallpox. On that day, the last natural case of smallpox developed. The patient with the symptoms was a hospital cook from Merca, Somalia, named Ali Maow

Figure 8.1 Ali Maow Maalin (pictured here) had the last natural case of smallpox (variola minor) in the world. Maalin, a hospital cook, was diagnosed with smallpox in Merca, Somalia, on October 26, 1977. Although he had contact with 161 people while infected, none of them developed the disease, thus ending the chain of transmission.

Maalin. Maalin recovered and became the world's last known smallpox case (Figure 8.1).

After Maalin recovered and none of his contacts developed the disease, the World Health Organization (WHO) reacted swiftly to the wonderful news. It recommended that smallpox vaccinations cease and that the number of laboratories studying smallpox virus be reduced. Countries throughout the world were quick to comply with both recommendations. Indeed, before smallpox eradication, 76 medical research facilities had stocks of smallpox virus, but by the end of 1978, that number had decreased to 12 (the Birmingham laboratory was one of those 12).

Further reductions in smallpox stocks occurred in the following years as the WHO encouraged countries to destroy their stocks or ship them to one of two repositories: the Centers for Disease Control and Prevention (CDC) in Atlanta, Georgia, or the Research Institute for Viral Preparations in Moscow, Russia. Japan sent its stocks to the CDC in 1979, the Netherlands did likewise in 1981, and England did so in 1982. Brazil, Botswana, India, Indonesia, and Pakistan sent theirs to Moscow. The last country to comply was South Africa. Amid much fanfare, it destroyed its remnants of smallpox virus in 1983. Now, only these laboratories in the United States and Russia have smallpox stocks, with about 400 strains in the United States and 200 strains in Russia.

It was apparent that the battle against smallpox had been won. However, the remnants of the viral army still existed in two

THE CENTERS FOR DISEASE CONTROL AND PREVENTION (CDC)

The CDC is an agency of the United States Department of Health and Human Services. Headquartered in Atlanta, Georgia, the CDC has more than 8,500 employees charged with protecting the public's health. They do this by monitoring and investigating disease outbreaks, developing and advocating public health policy, and providing leadership and training in various areas of public health. The CDC works closely with state and international health agencies to achieve its goals.

laboratories. Suppose the virus somehow escaped? Or suppose it was used as a weapon of biowarfare? The dilemma was clear—should the last remaining stocks be destroyed?

DEBATING THE ISSUES

Janet Parker's fatal illness and its tragic consequences ignited the debate on whether smallpox was really gone or simply lying in wait, ready to attack an unprotected population if it were ever accidentally or intentionally released from storage. It was clear that the real danger lay not in nature, but with the remaining virus stocks in laboratories. In December 1990, this realization led the WHO, the United States, and the Soviet Union (as it was known at the time) to jointly agree that it was appropriate to destroy the last remaining stocks of virus. The proposed date of destruction was December 1993.

But not all scientists were in agreement with the decision. When surveyed in a 1986 poll by the WHO, some scientists asserted that the risk of keeping smallpox virus locked away was negligible. Others maintained that the smallpox virus should continue to be studied because this virus is unique among other viral groups; for example, smallpox virus has more DNA in its genome than any other virus and its replication patterns are unique (as discussed in Chapter 5).

Then there is the issue of finality. To some scientists, destroying the smallpox virus is the culmination of the effort to eradicate smallpox. However, other scientists argued that the destruction should be delayed because the virus could not be brought back if a reason for studying it emerged. This argument lost some of its weight in the early 1990s, when an effort began to determine the base sequence of the 186 kilobases in the smallpox virus genome. Although scientists could theoretically re-create the virus once its genetic base sequence was known, the task would be difficult because the virus is so complex.

The finality issue also applies to unknown viral samples. How can we be sure, one scientist argues, that overlooked vials of smallpox virus do not exist among the cobwebs of laboratory corners or forgotten at the bottoms of laboratory freezers? Moreover, it is possible that smallpox virus is still whole and active in the scars of pox victims buried in regions where their bodies do not decay, such as the permafrost areas of Russia. Or, could smallpox reemerge through the closely related disease monkeypox (discussed further in Chapter 10)? Given these circumstances, researchers maintain that the stocks should be retained for study.

Those arguing against destruction indicated that the slight risk of the virus escaping is outweighed by the wealth of scientific information that can still be gleaned from research—information about the intense virulence of the smallpox virus, its mechanisms for causing disease, and its use for screening drugs that might be used to destroy it. Opponents, however, suggested that the containment facilities necessary for smallpox research are so cumbersome and expensive that little research would be performed. Therefore, the stocks might as well be destroyed. However, some ecologists point out that destroying the virus would constitute the first deliberate extinction of a biological species, setting a dangerous precedent.

As December 1993 approached, it was clear that consensus on destroying smallpox stocks could not be reached. Not only were opinions heavily divided, but also, the technicality of obtaining permissions from all the countries storing their smallpox virus stocks in the United States or Russia loomed large. Thus, the WHO panel in charge of making the decision decided to delay the destruction until June 30, 1995. Eventually, heeding the advice of many nations of the world, the WHO panel also let this date pass by.

THE DEBATE CONTINUES

As the second half of the 1990s unfolded, a new issue relating to virus destruction surfaced: Defense agencies in several nations began to feel uneasy about the potential use of smallpox as a weapon in bioterrorism. During those years, Soviet defector

Ken Alibeck painted a somber picture of the Soviet efforts to develop and use smallpox virus as an agent of biowarfare. Other intelligence sources related that smallpox virus might exist in other laboratories in the world besides those in the United States and Russia. These and other factors prompted nations to begin researching protective measures against smallpox.

But the WHO was not ready to abandon the idea of destroying all smallpox virus stocks. In 1996, a scientific advisory board of the WHO voted unanimously to destroy the stocks (citing a "duty to public trust"), and the WHO set another "final" deadline of June 30, 1999. Approval soon came from the 190 member nations of the World Health Assembly, the parent organization of the WHO, and the destruction appeared certain.

However, nothing is certain when so many member nations must agree on an issue, and smallpox destruction proved to be no exception. In the three years between 1996 and 1999, the debate became heated as both sides argued their cases. By that time, the complete nucleotide sequences of several strains of smallpox virus were known, and those who advocated destroying the virus stocks claimed that they could re-create smallpox virus for research purposes by working with its DNA. Of course, they had not done so yet, and those who advocated saving the stocks pushed to keep the intact viruses to study their pathological effects and help understand how other viruses act as well. But, the destructionist camp wrote, the virus would wreak havoc on the world's population if it were released, especially since more and more people became susceptible to the disease with the demise of vaccination programs. The monkeypox outbreak in the Congo in 1996 was symbolic of what could happen.

Then there is the issue of example. Advocates of destruction maintained that destroying the stocks would send the clear signal that working with intact smallpox virus was considered illegal. Regrettably, the opponents pointed out, setting a good example would probably do little to prevent criminal activity.

As the June 1999 destruction date neared, science mixed with politics, and United States President Bill Clinton requested that the United States Institute of Medicine (IOM) examine the issue. It prepared a report entitled *Assessment of Future Scientific Needs for Live Variola Virus*. Though silent on whether or not the stocks should be destroyed, the report concluded that the most compelling need for long-term retention of the virus would be to study new antiviral agents and vaccines to protect against the accidental or intentional release of the virus. Clearly, the heightened anxiety about using smallpox virus as an agent of bioterrorism heavily influenced the IOM's report. By that time, the clandestine biowarfare facilities in the former Soviet Union were well known.

In April 1999, President Clinton took action. He signed a memorandum indicating that the United States would not destroy its viral stocks. (Russia indicated support for this decision. By that time, the Russian stocks had been moved to

WHO'S WHO?

Prominent scientists have lined up on both sides of the destruction argument. On the "destroyer" side are D.A. Henderson and Frank Fenner, leaders in the efforts that led to smallpox eradication. Others in the "destroyer" camp include Brian Mahy, former director of the Division of Viral and Rickettsial Diseases at the CDC and now at the National Center for Infectious Diseases; and Dmitry Lvov, director of the Ivanovsky Institute of Virology, Moscow, Russia.

The "preservers" include Wolfgang Joklik, emeritus professor of microbiology at Duke University; Bernard Moss, chief of the Laboratory of Viral Diseases at the National Institutes of Health; and L.S. Sandakhchiev, director of the State Research Center of Virology and Biotechnology, VECTOR in Russia.

Clearly, this dilemma, with eminent scholars/scientists on both sides, will be difficult to resolve.

the Russian State Centre for Research on Virology and Bio-technology in Koltsovo in the Novosibirsk Region of Siberia.) Administration officials cited the threat of bioterrorism as a determining factor and the need to conduct research for new treatments and preventive measures. Many of the traditional arguments for preserving the stocks were also cited.

The World Health Organization was quick to follow the lead of the United States. On May 24, 1999, the WHO adopted a resolution calling for a delay in the destruction of known stocks of smallpox virus. The delay is still in effect.

In the political climate that followed the terrorist attacks on the United States in September 2001, President George W. Bush more rigidly focused the terms for the destruction of smallpox virus stocks. In November 2001, the Bush administration specified that the following four criteria must be met before the United States will consider destroying its stocks of smallpox virus:

- A new, safe (for all) vaccine with limited side effects must be developed,

- Two antiviral medications must be identified and produced,

- Quick, reliable diagnostic tests must be developed, and

- The ability to defeat genetically altered versions of the virus must be developed.

Given these criteria and the recent outbreaks of monkey-pox in the United States (spring 2003), it seems unlikely that destruction of stocks will occur in the near future, if ever.

9

The Bioweapons Threat

The use of biological agents as weapons of war is not unheard of in human history. Because the human race could be devastated by such an attack, world governments have long since realized that nations need to agree to ban the use of these weapons.

THE GENEVA PROTOCOL

Following World War I, as part of the Treaty of Versailles, Germany was forbidden to use bioweapons of any kind. In addition, by signing the Geneva Protocol, 29 countries agreed to ban the "use in war of asphyxiating, poisonous or other gases and of all analogous liquids, materials or devices." The Protocol goes on to extend this prohibition to the use of bacteriological methods of warfare (Figure 9.1).

Although the Geneva Protocol was an admirable attempt to limit the use and proliferation of poisonous gases and germ warfare, the agreement, through poor choice of words and omission, had limited impact. The Protocol unfortunately banned only the "first use" of a weapon, not production or research. Also, it made no provision for inspections or verification of compliance and spoke only to the use of bacteria as weapons while ignoring viruses and fungal pathogens. It is interesting to note that, in the years following its signing in 1925 and its ratification in 1926, 43 more countries signed the document; however, neither Japan nor the United States signed the agreement until the 1970s.

BIOWEAPONS USE AND RESEARCH

Notable use and testing of bioweapons by various nations are numerous. Japan carried out experiments with biowarfare during World War II. Its

PROTOCOL FOR THE PROHIBITION OF THE USE IN WAR OF ASPHYXIATING, POISONOUS OR OTHER GASES, AND OF BACTERIOLOGICAL METHODS OF WARFARE

Signed at Geneva June 17, 1925
Entered into force February 8, 1928
Ratification advised by the U.S. Senate December 16, 1974
Ratified by U.S. President January 22, 1975
U.S. ratification deposited with the
Government of France April 10, 1975
Proclaimed by U.S. President April 29, 1975

The Undersigned Plenipotentiaries, in the name of their respective Governments:

Whereas the use in war of asphyxiating, poisonous or other gases, and of all analogous liquids, materials or devices, has been justly condemned by the general opinion of the civilized world; and

Whereas the prohibition of such use has been declared in Treaties to which the majority of Powers of the World are Parties; and

To the end that this prohibition shall be universally accepted as a part of International Law, binding alike the conscience and the practice of nations;

Declare:

That the High Contracting Parties, so far as they are not already Parties to Treaties prohibiting such use, accept this prohibition, agree to extend this prohibition to the use of bacteriological methods of warfare and agree to be bound as between themselves according to the terms of this declaration.

The High Contracting Parties will exert every effort to induce other States to accede to the present Protocol. Such accession will be notified to the Government of the French Republic, and by the latter to all signatory and acceding Powers, and will take effect on the date of the notification by the Government of the French Republic.

The present Protocol, of which the French and English texts are both authentic, shall be ratified as soon as possible. It shall bear today's date.

The ratifications of the present Protocol shall be addressed to the Government of the French Republic, which will at once notify the deposit of such ratification to each of the signatory and acceding Powers.

The instruments of ratification of and accession to the present Protocol will remain deposited in the archives of the Government of the French Republic.

The present Protocol will come into force for each signatory Power as from the date of deposit of its ratification, and, from that moment, each Power will be bound as regards other powers which have already deposited their ratifications.

IN WITNESS WHEREOF the Plenipotentiaries have signed the present Protocol.

DONE at Geneva in a single copy, this seventeenth day of June, One Thousand Nine Hundred and Twenty-Five.

Figure 9.1 The Geneva Protocol was formulated in response to the terrible consequences of the use of poisonous gas in World War I. Originally signed by 29 countries, neither the United States nor Japan ratified the protocol until the 1970s. The Geneva Protocol served as a template for the formulation of the Biological Weapons Convention of 1972.

Special Army Unit 731, led by General Shihro Ishii, carried out a military campaign on civilians and prisoners of war in Manchuria using the agents of smallpox, plague, anthrax, and typhus.

During the Cold War, the United States tested open-air releases of the organisms causing brucellosis, tularemia, plague, and Q fever. By 1969, the United States had amassed a bioweapons store of 40,000 liters of antipersonnel bioweapons and 5 tons of anti-plant bioweapons. Research also focused on developing novel, antibiotic-resistant pathogens including a dispersible (without a live host) smallpox virus. President Richard Nixon terminated the United States' offensive bioweapons program in 1969; however, the defensive side of the program, including development of vaccines, was maintained.

During the Cold War, the Soviet bioweapons program was called Biopreparat. This program supported 40 facilities and employed approximately 30,000 scientists, engineers, and technicians. It operated on a budget of approximately $1 billion, which permitted research on 37 select organisms, including viruses such as Marburg, hantavirus, yellow fever, and influenza. Bacterial pathogens included organisms causing anthrax, plague, tularemia, cholera, and typhoid fever.

As part of Biopreparat, the Soviets conducted open-air testing on Vozrozhdeniye Island in the Aral Sea. These field tests began in 1936 and continued until, at best estimate, 1992. Smallpox virus, the anthrax-causing bacterium, and other organisms were tested on animals, plants, and livestock on the island. The goal of this program was to develop pathogens resistant to ultraviolet light, temperature, heat, and radiation. As the Aral Sea continues to shrink due to years of poor irrigation practices, the water barrier between Vozrozhdeniye Island and the mainland is slowly diminishing. Some scientists fear that the biological agents used there will no longer remain isolated (Figure 9.2).

Figure 9.2 Spanning both Uzbekistan and Kazakhstan (part of the former Soviet Union), the Aral Sea has undergone dramatic changes in the past 30 years. Volume has decreased by 75%, surface area by 50% and sea level has fallen by 16 meters. During winter, ice sheet formation almost links Vozrozhdeniye Island (arrow) to the mainland. Ice bridges and retreating waters have raised concerns that previously isolated biological agents tested on the island could be transmitted to the mainland.

While the United States' and Soviet programs were known, much concern among the world's nations today revolves around the unknown. Do other countries or terrorist groups intend to use bioweapons? Have former Soviet scientists living in a poor Russian economy sold biological agents or their knowledge about them to the highest bidder? Clearly, all of the ramifications of this escalating problem must be addressed openly, very soon.

BIOLOGICAL WEAPONS CONVENTION

On March 26, 1975, the United Nations General Assembly held the first Biological Weapons Convention (BWC). Although all members of the United Nations Security Council and 144 interested parties attended the conference, notably missing were representatives from Israel, Egypt, Syria, Sudan, and Algeria. At the convention, participating countries agreed to not produce, acquire, or attain bioweapons, including any that might be produced in the future. Unfortunately, this group repeated the mistakes of the Geneva Protocol signed 50 years prior, and failed to include any provisions regarding inspection, enforcement, or sanctions.

Although the traditional superpowers, the United States and Russia, have renounced their efforts to sustain inventories of bioweapons, rogue states or terrorist groups are now of great concern. In 1994, President Bill Clinton declared a national state of emergency relating to the spread of weapons of mass destruction (WMD), asserting that the potential use of WMD by a terrorist group or rogue state constitutes "an unusual and extraordinary threat to the national security, foreign policy and economy of the United States."

In a speech given by John R. Bolton at the 5th Biological Weapons Convention Review Conference Meeting in 2001, the United States publicly accused five countries (North Korea, Iraq, Iran, Libya, and Syria) of violating the BWC and hinted that other nations could readily be added to the roster of nations preparing for illicit germ warfare.

By December 2001, the discussion reached an impasse when President George W. Bush's administration declared opposition to recent convention compromises and asserted that the convention failed to provide a sufficient inspection procedure, and that certain intrusions could compromise industrial secrets in the biotech industry. The Johns Hopkins–based working group on civilian biodefense has stated that "its [bioweapons] potential for devastation today is far greater than at any previous time."

THE FEAR BECOMES REALITY

In October 2001, the first case of inhalational anthrax was reported in an office worker in Florida. Initially, the report raised few alarms, although no anthrax cases had been reported in the United States since 1976. Over the next six weeks, 21 additional cases in seven states along the East Coast were reported. Ten of these cases were inhalational and 11 of them were infections of the skin, the cutaneous form of anthrax. Five of the inhalational cases were lethal. Ninety-one percent of those infected were either postal workers or had been in environments where mail was handled. The infectious material was tracked to envelopes that had been loaded with *Bacillus anthracis* spores. Four of the envelopes were mailed in or around Trenton, New Jersey. By the time the anthrax threat passed, the U.S. House of Representatives had been shut down, mailrooms were abandoned, major media in New York and Florida had been victimized, and everyone was looking closely at their mail. Overwhelmed state and county health departments were dealing with false alarms as well as inadequate and slow testing of potential samples, and physicians were being deluged with requests from patients for the antibiotic ciprofloxacin. To date, no person or group has been implicated or come forward to claim responsibility for this act of terror. Considering the havoc the incident wreaked, there is clearly a need to organize and prepare the country for a better response if and when we are confronted by bioweapons again.

WHY USE BIOWEAPONS?

Perhaps the primary attraction of bioweapons is that they are accessible. Many of the organisms are found in nature, and are available either commercially (see the box on the following page) or on the black market. It is easy and inexpensive to build facilities in which to prepare weapons-grade material. Although some scientific knowledge is required, technical expertise is not necessary to develop these weapons and aerial delivery systems are easy to establish.

Fortunately, the smallpox virus is not the best choice as a bioweapon for the following reasons:

- The disease has a long incubation period, which would allow an outbreak to be spotted, patients isolated, and contacts vaccinated before the disease began to take its toll on the targeted population.

- A protective vaccine is available that may be given up to four days after exposure and still prevent disease.

- The virus can be difficult to manipulate to make it effective as a weapon.

- It is extremely difficult to obtain smallpox stocks because they are not available in nature or commercially.

Given the experience with anthrax in 2001, it seems that the use of bioweapons is a sure way to induce terror and gain an advantage over perceived or real enemies. However, considering how long they have been around, the use of bioweapons is rare because bioweapons have their drawbacks. Many biological weapons are hard to manufacture, particularly at the level of weapons-grade material where some bioagents may be unstable. Upon release of bioweapons, dispersion patterns

BIOWEAPONS THREAT

In 1995, Larry Wayne Harris of Lancaster, Ohio, was arrested when trying to purchase *Yersinia pestis*, the causative agent of plague. Although he placed the order without trouble, people at the company became concerned when he called repeatedly to check on the delivery date of his order. Harris, a trained microbiologist and alleged neo-Nazi, was arrested again three years later after attempting to purchase military-grade anthrax.

can be unpredictable because they are vulnerable to weather conditions and human behavior. Fear of blowback, when materials from the intended target make their way back to the country or perpetrator of the act, can also be a strong deterrent.

Given our experience with anthrax and now monkeypox (further discussed in Chapter 10), it is clear that a defense strategy for combating bioweapons is still underdeveloped. However, the problem has been identified and a willingness to confront the issue is clear. Establishment of the Department of Homeland Security and the federal plan for smallpox vaccination are first steps to combat the threat.

10

New Concerns and Future Prospects

A NEW POX ON OUR HOUSES

Monkeypox, a rare viral disease previously reported only in central and western Africa until 2003, was first identified in 1958 in a group of **cynomolgus** monkeys in a laboratory. Although called "monkeypox," the name is a misnomer, as the virus primarily infects rodents, with squirrels acting as the most likely major source of infection.

The orthopoxvirus causing monkeypox was not thought to be a threat to humans until the first human case was described in 1970 in Liberia, on the western coast of Africa. This outbreak aroused considerable concern in the public health community because 10% of the people infected died from the disease. This death rate is similar to the human death rate of some natural outbreaks of smallpox.

WHAT IS MONKEYPOX?

Monkeypox is a viral disease caused by an orthopoxvirus. It is a close relative of variola, the smallpox virus. The disease in humans is very similar to smallpox, with an incubation period of 12 to 14 days followed by fever, headache, muscle aches, and backache. Sore throat is also present and the rash and pocks that eventually develop are very similar to smallpox. The one minor difference between monkeypox and smallpox is the notable swollen lymph nodes that occur during monkeypox infection.

When attempting to diagnose monkeypox, the laboratory may try to isolate the virus from the patient in culture, identify it based upon its genetic makeup, or attempt to microscopically identify the virus by its appearance in lesions.

MONKEYPOX BECOMES MORE COMMON

Another large outbreak of monkeypox occurred over a five-year period beginning in 1981 in the Republic of Congo (formerly Zaire). By 1986, WHO had investigated 338 cases of monkeypox, with a mortality rate of approximately 10%. The Congolese, however, were not overly concerned because monkeypox was considered a small threat compared to other major disease problems in the country, including HIV/AIDS, malaria, and tuberculosis.

Ten years later, citizens of the Congo were struck again. Between February 1996 and February 1997, the Republic of Congo reported 92 cases of monkeypox, with three resulting in death. Notably, 73% of those infected were infected by other people rather than through animal contact. Previously, it had been thought that human-to-human transmission was limited to less than 30% of the total cases. During this outbreak, one patient was believed to have passed the virus to eight other people. This was a very high and previously undescribed rate of transmission.

Why was monkeypox now occurring regularly in the Congo and why did it seem to be increasing in its rates of virulence and transmission? Several explanations have been put forth. During the 1996 outbreak in Congo, the country was engaged in a civil war. Civilians fleeing rebel troops were threatened with starvation, so they hunted animals like small rodents, squirrels, and monkeys, which put them in greater contact with these animals and at greater risk for contracting monkeypox. Another explanation for the increasing reports of monkeypox is that since humans are no longer vaccinated against smallpox, their immunity has waned to both smallpox and monkeypox (the vaccine protects against both diseases).

And finally, some scientists suggest that the monkeypox virus has somehow mutated and is now more infectious, transmissible, and deadly to humans. Although this explanation is the most frightening of the three, it is also the least likely; there is no evidence that the virus has mutated. Partial sequence analysis of the strains found in two separate outbreaks of monkeypox (1970 and 1996) confirms that the virus has not changed genetically.

MONKEYPOX ARRIVES IN THE UNITED STATES

In the spring of 2003, several cases of a pox-type disease appeared in residents of Wisconsin. A common thread in all cases was that those affected were either owners of prairie dogs or had contacts with owners of prairie dogs. The diagnosis as monkeypox was eventually confirmed. It was believed that the prairie dogs had been infected by imported Gambian giant pouched rats (Figure 10.1).

As of June 25, 2003, a total of 79 cases were reported over a 2-month period in 6 Midwest states (Figure 10.2). To prevent further transmission of monkeypox, 26 people who came into contact with the infected individuals were vaccinated with smallpox vaccine. No deaths resulted from this outbreak, and 35% of the confirmed cases had previously been vaccinated against smallpox. As a result of the outbreak, a legal embargo on certain animals has been put in place by the federal government. Prairie dogs and six other exotic animals were banned for importation.

THE FUTURE

Given the uncertainty of the use of smallpox virus as a bioweapon, our concern regarding its possession by rogue states, the stay of execution for remaining stocks, and the emergence of monkeypox, it is difficult to predict what the future holds for smallpox.

Figure 10.1 Imported Gambian giant pouched rats (shown here) are believed to have transmitted the monkeypox virus to prairie dogs. These prairie dogs, purchased as pets, transmitted the virus to their owners, resulting in the first recorded outbreak of monkeypox in the United States in the spring of 2003.

The 2002 federal plan to vaccinate 5 to 10 million United States citizens against smallpox has not materialized. Unanticipated side effects of the smallpox vaccine have caused civilians and some scientists to question the need to vaccinate in an age of unknown risk. When severe acute respiratory syndrome (SARS) appeared in the fall of 2002, the world's attention focused on this new microbial foe to combat. Because the search in Iraq for weapons of mass destruction (including bioweapons) has, to date, not uncovered a verifiable threat, the public is less likely to consider the threat of smallpox a primary concern—which it may not be.

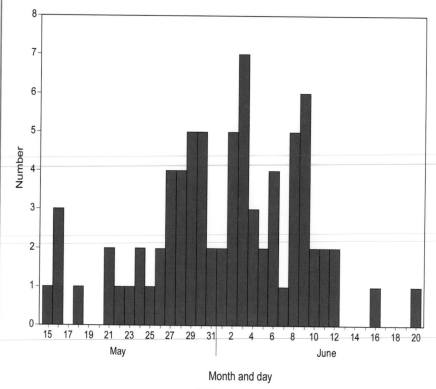

Number* of persons with monkeypox, by date of first symptom onset — Illinois, Indiana, Kansas, Missouri, Ohio, and Wisconsin, May 15–June 20, 2003

*N = 77. Includes laboratory-confirmed cases and cases under investigation. Dates of illness onset were not available for two patients.

Figure 10.2 This graph shows the number of individuals diagnosed with monkeypox in the United States during May and June 2003. The total number of cases identified was 79.

When Dr. D.A. Henderson, former chief of the WHO Intensified Eradication Program, spoke about smallpox at the American Society for Microbiology meeting in Washington,

D.C., in May 2003, he mentioned "chapters not yet written." Although we do not know what the future holds and the last chapters of the smallpox saga have yet to be written, let us hope that they are, as Henderson stated, "few and brief."

Glossary

Acute—Having rapid onset, developing quickly, and lasting for a relatively short (weeks as opposed to months) period of time (when discussing a disease).

Agar media—Artificial medium containing the necessary nutrients to grow bacteria and fungi. The solidifying agent is agar, a compound derived from seaweed.

Amino acids—The building blocks of protein. There are 20 recognized naturally occurring amino acids.

Animal reservoir—Animals (other than humans) that provide a continual source of infectious agents.

Antibody, antibodies—Protective proteins produced in response to a specific antigen. An antibody combines with that specific antigen to produce an antibody/antigen complex.

Antigen—Cellular or viral components that induce a specific host immune response.

Antigenically—Of or concerning the antigenic makeup.

Bacterium—A prokaryotic, single-celled organism.

B cells—Lymphocyte that matures in the bone marrow and other lymphoid tissue. B cells differentiate into plasma cells, which produce protective proteins called antibodies.

Bifurcated—Two-pronged. The type of needle used to introduce vaccinia virus into the skin.

Bioterrorists, bioterrorism—Individuals or groups with extreme beliefs who would use biological agents or compounds to kill or cause harm to others who do not share like ideologies.

Budding—The process whereby viruses leave the host cell. The virus acquires the envelope from the host cell in this process.

Buffer—A suspending liquid that prevents wide swings in the acid-base balance of a solution.

Capsid—The protein component surrounding the viral genetic material. The organization of the capsid establishes the shape of the virus.

Carrier—An individual harboring an infectious agent yet showing no signs or symptoms of disease. A carrier can unknowingly transmit the infectious agent.

Cell—The basic unit of biological systems. Cells are microscopic, reproduce, and have a double-layered membrane that allows them to regulate interior conditions.

Cell-mediated arm—The part of the immune response that involves the actions of T cells.

Complement—A series of 20 serum proteins that, once activated by an antibody/antigen complex, form a cascade that ultimately results in the destruction of viral infected cells.

Conjunctiva—Membranes of the eye that line the inner surface of the eyelid and cover the front part of the white of the eye.

Containment—Along with surveillance, part of the smallpox eradication strategy involving isolation of affected individuals as well as their contacts. All contacts were then vaccinated to "contain" the outbreak.

Cynomolgus—A small, short-tailed monkey native to southeastern Asia, Borneo, and the Philippines that is often used in medical research.

Cytokines—Small proteins produced by one cell, often T cells and macrophages, that influence other cells, especially T cells. Some examples of cytokines include interferons and interleukins.

Cytoplasm—Everything inside the cell, excluding the nucleus.

Cytotoxic T cells—T-lymphocytes that target and destroy viral-infected host cells.

DNA—Deoxyribonucleic acid, the genetic material of cells. Defined segments of DNA are called genes.

Eczema—A skin condition of unknown cause characterized initially by swelling, redness, weeping, and the presence of small blisters. The condition eventually progresses resulting in crusty, scaly, and thickened skin.

Electron microscopy—Type of microscopy that uses electrons to illuminate details of a specimen. Electron microscopes can achieve magnifications of 100,000X and resolve structures as small as 2 nanometers (a nanometer equals 10^{-9} meter).

Endemic—Referring to the incidence of disease in a population, a small number of cases occurring regularly throughout the year in a particular geographical area.

Envelope—A host-derived layer surrounding the viral capsid.

Enzyme—A protein that serves as a biological catalyst to drive chemical reactions in living systems.

Epidermis—The outer layer of the skin.

Glossary

Eradication—Total destruction or elimination from existence.

Family—A taxonomic group. Organisms that share several characteristics and are more similar than members of a kingdom and phylum, but not as closely related as members of a genus, are considered a family.

Firewall—A barrier that is impenetrable.

Genetic diversity—Genetic variation within a group. As far as evolution and natural selection are concerned, genetic diversity is a positive characteristic for a population.

Genome—The genetic information contained within an organism.

Genus—A taxonomic group. Members of the same genus are closely related species.

Golgi bodies—Membrane-bound structures of the eukaryotic cell that are involved in the modification and transport of protein.

Icosahedron—A geometric shape with 20 triangular sides.

Immune complexes—Antigen and antibody complexes (precipitates or agglutinates) that are usually cleared from the body by phagocytic cells.

Immune response—The action of specific immune cells and the release of chemicals in response to recognition of antigen.

Immunity—A state of protection or resistance to a specific pathogen.

Infection clusters—Group of individuals in a specific area with a particular infectious disease.

Inoculation—Injection or purposeful introduction of an infectious agent into a host, usually with the goal of producing an immune response.

Interferon—Antiviral proteins produced by the cell in response to viral infection. These nonspecific cytokines will protect adjacent cells from viral infection.

Kilobase—1,000 bases. Bases are the nitrogen-containing compounds, (adenine, thymine, guanine, cytosine, uracil [A,T,G,C,U] that are part of a nucleotide, which is the basic unit of genetic material [DNA or RNA]). A kilobase is the unit commonly used to describe the size of a genome.

Lesions—Eruptions, disruptions, or other abnormality on the skin.

Lymph—A thin, clear, pale yellow fluid that circulates in the lymphatic vessels and is filtered by the lymph nodes. Lymph, which is 95% water, contains a few red blood cells as well as white blood cells.

Lyse—To break open.

Lysosomes—Enzyme-containing structures in eukaryotic cells. The contents of a lysosome are often used to destroy invading infectious agents.

Macules—Lesions that appear at the beginning of the smallpox rash. Macules appear as tiny pink to red dots.

Memory—The second and each subsequent time the host is exposed to a specific antigen, the immune response will be more rapid and intensified due to the presence of memory cells that are primed and ready to respond.

Messenger RNA—A type of nucleic acid that holds the information necessary to create a string of amino acids that will eventually function as protein.

Microbes—Microorganisms including viruses, bacteria, protists, and fungi.

Mitochondria—Structures found in eukaryotic organisms responsible for generating energy for the host cell.

Mucous membranes—The moist openings or canals of the body, including the nose, mouth, digestive tract, reproductive tract, and urinary tract.

Mutate—A permanent change in the genetic information of an organism. Mutation may occur spontaneously, or be induced by environmental mutagens.

Natural selection—Process in which environmental pressure selects for those individuals having the genetic makeup that will allow them to survive and reproduce in the changing environment.

Nucleocapsid—In a virus, the genetic material and surrounding protein capsid.

Nucleotide—The basic building block of genetic material (DNA or RNA) composed of a 5-carbon sugar, phosphate, and a nitrogen-containing base.

Nucleus—Structure in a eukaryotic cell that includes the genetic material surrounded by a double-layered membrane.

Papules—The second stage of the smallpox rash, which appears as pink pimples.

Parasitism—Relationship in which a microbe harms the host organism or cell.

Phagocytosis, phagocytic cells—Ingestion of solids, or the name for "eating" cells such as neutrophils and macrophages responsible for removing (and killing, if necessary) organisms and debris from the body.

Phenol—A chemical derived from coal or plant tar used for preserving solutions. Phenol kills and prevents the growth of bacteria and fungi by injuring their plasma membranes, which results in the leakage of the cells' cytoplasm.

Glossary

Primary cell cultures—Cell cultures created using the tissue directly from animals; these cell cultures can only be maintained for a short period of time.

Pustules—Lesions of the smallpox rash that appear as small raised bumps filled with pus.

Replication—To reproduce, increase in number, or make more of oneself.

Ribosome—Structures in both prokaryotic and eukaryotic cells that participate in the production of protein from an RNA template.

RNA—Ribonucleic acid. Genetic material composed of ribose, phosphate and nitrogenous bases (A,U,G,C). RNA may function as messenger RNA, transfer RNA, or ribosomal RNA.

RNA polymerase—An enzyme responsible for the production of RNA from a DNA template.

Scourge—A cause of great suffering, affliction, or destruction.

Secondary diploid cell lines—The cells that develop when one type of cell from the primary cell culture is taken and cultured apart from other cells to obtain a set of genetically identical cells. These cells can be passed or subcultured up to approximately 50 times.

Strain—Organisms that are members of the same species but have minor genetic differences, producing a subgroup of the species.

Subcutaneous—Below the surface of the skin.

Surveillance—To monitor the incidence of disease. Part of the surveillance-containment strategy involving aggressive case hunting and detection of all cases of smallpox in an area.

T cells—A thymus-derived lymphocyte that functions in the cell-mediated arm of the immune response. T cells may function as killers (cytotoxic T cells), or produce various cytokines, which influence the activity of other cells.

Toxemia—The condition resulting when toxins are found in the blood, usually as a result of microbial infection.

Vaccine—Purposeful introduction of live, dead, or modified microorganisms or their products into a host to produce immunity to that microbe or its component.

Vaccinia—Another name for cowpox.

Variola minor—A less severe form of smallpox resulting in infection with approximately 1% mortality.

Variolation—Purposeful introduction of variola virus (smallpox virus) into the skin or vein to produce a mild case of smallpox, resulting in lifelong immunity to the virus.

Vesicles—Stage in the smallpox rash where lesions appear as small raised bumps.

Virion—A single viral particle.

Virus—A microscopic infectious agent composed of genetic material and a protein coat. Viruses can only replicate in the cells of other living organisms.

World Health Organization (WHO)—A public health organization of the United Nations headquartered in Geneva, Switzerland.

Further Reading

Bazin, Herve. *The Eradication of Smallpox*. San Diego: Academic Press, 2000.

Benbehani, Abbas M. "The Smallpox Story: Life and Death of an Old Disease." *Microbiological Reviews* 47 (1983): 455–509.

Brooks, George F., Janet S. Butel, and Stephen A. Morse. *Medical Microbiology*, 22nd ed. Stamford, CT: Appleton and Lange, 2000.

Cowley, Geoffrey. "The Plan to Fight Smallpox." *Newsweek* (October 14, 2002): 45–52.

Fenn, Elizabeth A. *Pox Americana, the Great Smallpox Epidemic of 1775–82*. New York: Hill and Wang, 2001.

Fenner, F., D.A. Henderson, I. Arita, Z. Jezek, and I.D. Ladnyi. *Smallpox and Its Eradication*. Geneva, Switzerland: World Health Organization, 1988.

Giblin, James Cross. *When Plague Strikes. The Black Death, Smallpox and AIDS*. New York: Harper Collins, 1995.

Hopkins, D.R. *Princes and Peasants: Smallpox in History*. Chicago: University of Chicago Press, 1983.

Joklik, W., B. Moss, B. Fields, D. Bishop, and L. Sandakhchiev. "Why the Smallpox Virus Should Not Be Destroyed." *Science* 262 (1993): 1225–1226.

Karlen, Arno. *Man and Microbes, Diseases and Plagues in History and Modern Times*. New York: G.P. Putnam's Sons, 1995.

Koplow, David. *Smallpox, the Fight to Eradicate a Global Scourge*. Berkeley, CA: University of California Press, 2003.

Mahy, B., J. Almond, K. Berns, R. Chanock, D. Lvov, R. Petterson, H. Schatzmayr, and F. Fenner. "The Remaining Stocks of Smallpox Virus Should Be Destroyed." *Science* 262 (1993): 1223–1224.

Miller, Judith, Stephen Engelberg, and William Broad. *Germs*. New York: Simon & Schuster, 2002.

Needham, Cynthia A., and Richard Canning. *Global Disease Eradication. The Race to Save the Last Child*. Washington, D.C.: ASM Press, 2003.

Plotkin, Stanley A., and Edward A. Mortimer Jr., eds. *Vaccines*, 2nd ed. Philadelphia: W. B. Saunders, 1994.

Websites

American Medical Association, Special Report on Smallpox
http://www.ama-assn.org/ama/pub/article/2036-7036.html

American Museum of Natural History:
"Epidemic, the World of Infectious Disease" Exhibition
http://www.amnh.org/exhibitions/epidemic/index.html

Armed Forces Institute of Pathology (U.S.), Information on Smallpox
http://www.afip.org/Departments/infectious/sp/text/1_1.htm

CDC Website with Smallpox Information
http://www.bt.cdc.gov/agent/smallpox/index.asp

Centers for Disease Control and Prevention (CDC)
www.cdc.gov

E Medicine Information on Smallpox
http://www.emedicine.com/emerg/topic885.htm

Infectious Disease Society of America, Bioterrorism
Information and Resources
http://vaccinationnews.com/DailyNews/October2002/Smallpox13.htm

Johns Hopkins, Center for Civilian Biodefense Strategies
http://www.hopkins-biodefense.org/index.html

Karolinska Institutet (Sweden) History of Disease Links
http://www.mic.ki.se/HistDis.html

Medline Plus, National Library of Medicine, Smallpox
http://www.nlm.nih.gov/medlineplus/smallpox.html

Poxvirus Bioinformatics Resource Center (Poxvirus genetic sequences)
http://www.poxvirus.org/index.html

UCLA Library Online: "Smallpox: Inoculation,
Vaccination, Eradication."
http://www.library.ucla.edu/libraries/biomed/smallpox/

Who Named It? (Enter "Jenner" or "Smallpox" in the search field)
http://www.whonamedit.com/

World Health Organization
www.who.int

World Health Organization Factsheet on Smallpox
http://www.who.int/emc/diseases/smallpox/factsheet.html

Index

Index

Picture Credits

11: Courtesy Public Health Image Library (PHIL), CDC
12: © Reuters NewMedia Inc. /CORBIS
15: Courtesy World Health Organization (WHO)
20: Courtesy WHO
22: © David Cumming; Eye Ubiquitous/CORBIS
28: © Bettmann/CORBIS
32: Library of Congress, LC-USZ62-12251
36: © Hulton-Deutsch Collection/CORBIS
39: National Library of Medicine
41: © CORBIS
42: (top) © Science VU/CDC/Visuals Unlimited
42: (bottom) © Dr. H. Gelderblom/Visuals Unlimited
45: Lambda Science Artwork

47: Lambda Science Artwork
49: Lambda Science Artwork
51: Courtesy PHIL, CDC
53: Lambda Science Artwork
58: Lambda Science Artwork
60: © Paul Almasy/CORBIS
68: Courtesy PHIL, CDC
70: Courtesy PHIL, CDC
71: Courtesy PHIL, CDC
75: Courtesy PHIL, CDC
85: Digital image © 1996 CORBIS; Original image courtesy of NASA/CORBIS
93: Associated Press, AP/Douglas C. Pizac
94: Courtesy Morbidity and Mortality Weekly Report (MMWR), CDC

Cover: © Science VU/CDC/Visuals Unlimited

About the Author

Kim R. Finer received her B.A. in microbiology at Miami University, and her Ph.D. in veterinary microbiology at Texas A&M University. She currently is an associate professor in the Department of Biological Sciences at Kent State University where she teaches courses in microbiology, human genetics, and ecology. She has written textbooks on the use of Internet resources in the classroom, and has published numerous papers in the areas of biology education as well as in her research area. She received the Exxon Foundation Innovation in Education Award in 1996, was elected to Who's Who Among America's Teachers in 1998, and was recently identified as a national model course developer by the SENCER program of the Association of American Colleges and Universities. She is currently serving as a Waksman Foundation lecturer and Microbiology Education Division chairperson for the American Society for Microbiology. Kim lives in Wooster, Ohio, with her two teenage children, Ben and Julia, her husband, John, and dog, Jenny.

About the Editor

The late I. Edward Alcamo was a Distinguished Teaching Professor of Microbiology at the State University of New York at Farmingdale. Alcamo studied biology at Iona College in New York and earned his M.S. and Ph.D. degrees in microbiology at St. John's University, also in New York. He had taught at Farmingdale for over 30 years. In 2000, Alcamo won the Carski Award for Distinguished Teaching in Microbiology, the highest honor for microbiology teachers in the United States. He was a member of the American Society for Microbiology, the National Association of Biology Teachers, and the American Medical Writers Association. Alcamo authored numerous books on the subjects of microbiology, AIDS, and DNA technology as well as the award-winning textbook *Fundamentals of Microbiology*, now in its sixth edition.